Observations in C Major
prose & poetry

Gerald Finlay

Copyright © Gerald Finlay 2008

The right of Gerald Finlay to be identified as the author of this work has been asserted in accordance with sections 77 and 78 of the Copyright, Designs and Patents Act 1988.

All rights reserved. No part of this publication may be reproduced, stored in or introduced into a retrieval system, or transmitted, in any form, or by any means without the prior written permission of the publisher.

This book is sold subject to the condition that it shall not, by way of trade or otherwise, be lent, resold, hired out, or otherwise circulated without the publisher's prior consent in any form of binding or cover other than that in which it is published and without a similar condition including this condition being imposed on the subsequent purchaser.

First published in Great Britain
by
SRE-F (Books) Hambleton, Selby
North Yorkshire UK.

CIP catalogue record for this book is available from the British Library

ISBN 978-0-9556817-4-5

Cover photographs by Gerald Finlay

Cover design by David Gardiner

Dedication

For Shirley and my family

About the Author

The author lives in North Yorkshire with his wife Shirley.
They have three children and five grandchildren.
Gerald is a retired medical engineer.

Also by this author:

'Orb Web Tales' (A collection of Short Stories)

ISBN: 978-0-9556817-1-4 (Hardback)

ISBN: 978-0-9556817-0-7 (Paperback)

Contents

Death and Aunt Maude	11
Six Haiku	14
The Curious Incident of the Cow in the Indian Daytime	15
Come Evil Bombs	19
The Legend of the Corryvreckan	20
Ockerlolly	22
This Thing in Front	26
Dante's Gate	27
A Very Greek Wedding	28
Sadie's Story	32
A Purple Skeleton	34
Scamp Writes to Australia	35
Good Friday in Los Gigantas	37
Eine Gnadige Frau mit Vielem Wind	38
And the Earth Moved	42
Graduation	45
Oliver Twist	46
Me and my Shadow	48
No Blandish for Miss Orchids	54
Closing Down Sale	56
1936 (MCMXXXVI)	57
Penance	63
I Sold the World	64
Journey's End	66
Too Long a Road	68
An Enigma	70
The Old Age Problem Sorted	71
Precious Memories	74
On a Wedding	75
A Young Boy's Memories of WW2	76

Ariadne	82
The Damsel	84
The Prison	85
The Long Trek	88
The Human Race	89
The Hymn of the Deaf Mutes	90
Stress and Beauty	93
Gentler Days	94
Dear Basil – Love Scamp	96
Morning Vignette	99
Ode to an L-Driver	100
Everyone	101
Rescue in the Dolomites	102
The Traveller	106
Potency – can you grasp it?	108
Tommy and the Tin	109
In an English Country Garden	111
The Arrival of Godot	112
Choices	115
Tommy's Funeral	116
The Lecture	117
Twenty-Two	121
The Painter	122
Tracy's Letter	123
Phthalo Blue	125
Musica et Lacrima	126
Perception	128
Endorphins	130
A Badge Too Far	132
Incident on a Caribbean Reef	134
The Scum's Party	136
Have You Ever Been Really Frightened?	138
Opportunities	140
Peace	141

Observations in C Major
prose & poetry

Death and Aunt Maude

Contrary to what they say –
I haven't really passed away,
My breathing stopped I know that's true,
And they didn't know just what to do.
The EEG thing showed no trace.
There was a deathly look upon my face.
Electric shocks? They gave me four,
They made me jump but nothing more.
And then at last they realised –
I was no more, I had demised.

No bright lights or heavenly choir,
No smell of brimstone or raging fire.
But as I looked down I could clearly see,
They had pulled a white sheet over me.
I saw Aunt Maude and Uncle Fred
Standing stiffly by my bed,
There were some tears, Fred's eyes were wet,
But none from Maude – at least not yet.

And then I started to drift away,
I knew for sure I couldn't stay,
I was so glad now, that I had believed
On that score I was sure relieved,
I knew if there was anything there
Surely I had earned a share.
So I ventured forth with head held high,
Not knowing when or where or why,
I had tried my best along life's grind,
And just hoped that my judges were feeling kind.

After a while as if out of a dream
The most amazing sight that could ever have been,
A lovely cottage and crystal pool I could see
Suddenly appearing in front of me.
At the door of the cottage a vision so fair,
Stood a naked lady with long flowing hair,
I had seen nothing to match her beauty before,
As I cautiously made my way to the door.

Her nakedness just didn't seem wrong,
Such beauty you just shouldn't hide,
Then she spoke to me in a silken voice,
'You should see my friends inside!'

Through the perfumed garden and birdsong path
I slowly made my way.
I would find out now, if I was destined for hell –
For I would be surely turned away.
I knew this was heaven as I went through the door
Four more gorgeous ladies – as naked as before
It was hard to believe, but I'd make a sure bet
That these girls were better than the one I first met.
No, that's not right, there just different you see,
All perfect, all lovely, and all are for me.

I knew I'd been good, But reward such as this?
My goodness, my goodness, what joy, oh what bliss!

After hours and hours of endless delight,
A tinkling bell brought me back from the night
Then naked through the gardens – without any care
And down to the pool, and bath-time to share.
A breakfast of fruit then caressed in the sun,
Oh wonder of wonder this is paradise come.

And then sometime later the first lady I saw,
Waved me towards her as she stood by the door
She looked rather sad, with something not right
As I slowly approached her magnificent sight.
'There has been a mistake, I'm afraid you can't stay
You have got here too early it seems,
The boss has just told me you have to go back,
Please remember us in your dreams'.
'I don't want to go back,
I just love it here,
This is where I must be,'
'Well I'm sorry my friend we love you too,
But I'm afraid it's not up to me.'

With much sadness and sorrow we said our goodbyes
It was breaking my heart to leave,
But reluctantly I reversed my steps
I would have a long time now to grieve.

Maybe this is what hell is about,
And I had possibly got it all wrong,
I hadn't been good enough at all
Had they just been stringing me along?

Then I heard a voice in the distance,
'Welcome back, welcome back' and a smile,
'My goodness you gave us a fright my friend
We had lost you there for a while.'

I am tormented now with my journey
Why didn't they just let me stay?
But I know without doubt in the back of my mind
I shall return to my cottage one day.
And I know my ladies will be waiting for me
With the same longing I'm having now,
So dry your tears now dear Uncle Fred,
And Aunt Maude – *'Sod off you old cow'*

Six Haiku

These Haikus are based on six strange but personal experiences.

Caribbean experience

Snorkel in warm pool
Coral snake swims up to me
With sly glance moves on

African Experience 1

Croc, mouth wide open
Gently lift front leg and touch
Axilla like ice

African Experience 2

Laze in the warm sun
Monitor lizard strolls past
Hold breath for a while

Dorset Experience

Morning run on hills
Adder rears in front of me
Run turns to high jump

Mexican moment

Lay on still water
Sting-ray wakes from sandy bed
Then gracefully flies

Dominican Republic Experience

Arm wrestling contest
Deep trouble no avoiding
Quick win fast exit

The Curious Incident of the Cow in the Indian Daytime

We opened our curtains that first morning to a delightful view, from our balcony it was about two hundred yards across a beautiful yellow sandy beach to the gently rolling breakers of the Arabian Sea. I took a pre-breakfast stroll across the sands to the sea, passing on route a notice board warning about swimming during the monsoon – this would be no problem to us, we were well clear of the season.

My wife and I didn't realise during our first breakfast about the importance of getting extra food and taking it out of the hotel with us, but we were soon to discover.

Prior to going on the beach that first morning we went for a stroll around the small local village. The first thing we encountered was a number of dogs. The dogs were friendly enough and enjoyed a pat but were obviously expecting a bit more. From that morning the village dogs enjoyed a decent breakfast – we served ourselves a little more in the restaurant, and ate a little less. The dogs greeted us with wagging tales every morning.

I was out for a pre-breakfast run one morning when I encountered an old Indian gentleman dressed in flowing robes and with a turban on his head, he was very grubby. Beside him on a short tether was an Indian buffalo. This animal was painted and adorned in a most artistic way. I stopped, and he greeted me in the Indian manner of hands together in front and bowing of head. He indicated to me that he was hungry by putting his hand up to his mouth. I indicated to him to stay where he was and ran back to the hotel. I picked up my camera and collected what food we had and returned. What surprised me was that when I gave him the food his first thought was for his animal – he fed the buffalo before eating anything himself. We looked after this guy whilst we were there, but more of that later.

On the beach that first morning Shirley and I were approached by a well dressed Indian gentleman, he introduced himself, and told us he was a professional massager with a degree from Bomsimlamgallabadistan University and would give us the best massage we had ever had. We agreed a fair price and indeed this guy was good, we both enjoyed our hour-long full body massage. An Indian lady who had been watching the proceedings approached us after the man had left counting his rupees and informed us that she was much better qualified that the man was and had a better degree. She was, she told us, a professor of massageology from the University of Bangaloreaggradehlistanibad, and could she massage us tomorrow, we had to give her a chance and indeed she was good. So we ended up with the man and the lady giving us massages on alternate days – everyone was happy.

One day a group of monks walked solemnly down to the water in full saffron flowing robes. They took their sandals off and paddled in the warm water. Before long they were splashing one another and obviously enjoying themselves. They then left the water and stood around talking. A couple of minutes later two of them took their robes off and in their under pants went into the sea and whooped with delight. The other two stood on the sand sharing the delight of their friends. We were wondering why only the two had gone in the sea, was this some religious thing for them? But soon the reason became clear. The two monks emerged from the sea and donned their robes; they then took their underpants off and handed them to the other two, who then replaced them in the sea. The poor guys only had two pair of under garments between them. They had a wonderful time though, and after their fun, they dressed and walked solemnly back up the beach in total silence.

We were also entertained by beach performers, these were obviously families, and usually consisted of mother and father, son and daughter. The children were only young, probably about ten or eleven (not always easy to tell) but they did amazing things. They constructed a tightrope and performed unbelievable acts on it. The children then did acrobatics on the sand and then did a disappearing trick, which was truly amazing.

On another occasion a class of young ladies accompanied by very strict teachers came down to the beach. They had obviously been given instructions that they only paddle. Well they did start off paddling – but thirteen to fourteen year old young ladies do not always do what they are told, and before long they were splashing one another. Shouting from the teachers at the girls to keep themselves dry just produced laughter from the girls, and in no time they were fully submerged in the sea all fully clothed. It was a group of happy girls who later walked back up the beach saturated to the skin, with their stern-faced sari clad teachers beside them. We had had an afternoon of excellent entertainment and laughter.

Umakant was the guy who looked after the hotel pool and we got friendly with him. He was soon to be married and quite excited about it. Because we were kind to him he insisted on bringing us a meal that his mother would prepare for us. Nothing would stop him. The meal arrived one day wrapped in a Times of India newspaper. Umakant with some delight told us it was his mother's favourite dish a 'cold fish curry'. Now we didn't want to be unkind to Umakant and after thanking him profusely we told him we would have to eat the meal in our hotel room to enjoy it to the full. We retired to our room and inspected the curry. It did look nice and had been prepared with obvious care, but we just dare not attempt any of it. Our plumbing of course is not up to eating the indigenous Indian style of cooking. The water has to be avoided at all costs; one only has to eat a small amount of the wrong thing and Bingo. The next morning I took the meal to my rendezvous with the old Indian gentleman and his buffalo – they shared the abundant food between them and both had a look of delight on their faces after they had finished. The food thankfully had not been wasted. Later that morning Umakant was eager to know how the food had been, we were able to tell him that his mother's cooking had been thoroughly enjoyed and every scrap eaten, he was delighted, and we didn't feel too bad about it.

But I digress – what has this to do with 'The Curious Incident of The Cow in the Daytime' I hear you ask. So I will now tell you about the said cow:

If one requires to buy gold or silver or jade, indeed anything of value in India then a town will have to be visited, only low-value trinkets and such can be bought locally or on the beach. This will then entail a journey of absolute terror. The only way to get to a town is by taxi or rickshaw. The taxi will be the less terrifying – but choose the rickshaw. The terror will last so much longer in the taxi and you will also be cooked alive, the air conditioning is an open window. You will also go deaf from the continuous sounding of the horn by the driver and also by every other driver. The rickshaw is motor driven and has only one speed: 'flat out'. These machines not only go round cars at either side, they can go under and over also. They never slow down – the driver is only thinking about one thing, his next fare. It is advisable before entering a rickshaw to make direct contact with your God, and to keep close contact with him or her throughout the journey. The only thing that will slow this infernal machine down is not the brakes (they don't have any!), it is the cow.

Just one other thing – only have about a hundred rupees in your bum bag. This is payment for the young dipper's professionalism. Believe me the money will have disappeared before you have gone a hundred yards and you will have no idea – no matter where your bum bag was! The only place to keep your money safe is in your hand or maybe down the front of your undergarment. These young guys are high-class operators.

Sorry, I digressed again.

Now back to the cow. In India the cow roams free, you will see them in the markets on the pavements on the streets and on the beach. Vehicles only stop for cows – not anything else. Crowds will part for a cow, not for anything else. Although I have never seen anyone act unkindly to a cow in India, I have never seen anyone act particularly kindly to one either, I am prepared to believe that some do though.

The Hindu gentle cow is considered sacred and thought to be a gift from the gods. To the Hindu the cow represents the divine mother that sustains all human beings.

Early on in our holiday in India, I think probably the second day, I was talking to one of the young Indians who sell trinkets on the beach, when this cow appeared and walked down towards the sea. I asked the girl where the cow was going. She told me that the cow was going to the waste bin to see if there was anything to eat. It was lunchtime and many people have bananas for lunch and put the skins in the bins. The cow apparently eats the skins. Now I got to thinking that if this poor cow had to eat banana skins it must be pretty hungry.

Shirley and I had just been to the local village and bought some bananas. We had a good breakfast each morning and only had a small snack at midday. I collected a handful of bananas and walked the couple of hundred yards to the cow. It looked at me with big doleful eyes and watched as I unzipped a banana, I then held it out and it gently took it from me and chewed it. I then gave it another, well it had the whole bunch and then ate the skins as well. It then gave me one last look before turning round and slowly walking off the beach. Bananas were quite cheap so we decided to buy a large bunch the next day and watch out to see if our new friend turned up again. Sure enough the cow was back the next day at the same time, this time I was waiting with the bananas.

It was about three o'clock I had just had a swim and was laid on my sun bed, Shirley was reading in the shade of the beach parasol. I heard someone shout, 'Look, look!' I turned around and stood behind my sun bed was the cow. Now how on earth had the cow found me? This was a very large beach with many people and many sun beds. The cow lay down beside me and went to sleep with me scratching its tummy. I kid you not. When it was time for us to go for our shower and prepare for the evening, the cow got up and strolled from the beach.

We didn't go to the same part of the beach every day, nor did we wear the same clothes. The cow always left the beach after I had fed it, and before I returned to my spot. Yet everyday that we were on the beach the cow found us and lay down beside us until we left. It was such a strange thing, the local folk couldn't understand it and told us they had never seen a cow get close to anyone, never mind finding someone on the large beach and then lying down with them, and letting itself be touched. The story soon got around and people were waiting for the cow to make its entry and find us. It became a celebrity cow – and many photos and film was taken of the cow heading towards Shirley and I and then lying down with us.

When we returned home I contacted Umerkant to send him a wedding present and to ask him about the cow. He told me that other than going to the bin for banana skins, the cow never made any attempt to go anywhere else on the beach after we had left India. I found that strangely moving.

I think that qualifies as a curious incident.

Come Evil Bombs

Any Similarity with a certain poem by JB is purely intentional.

Come evil bombs and fall on Britain
Not fit for decent people now
No one immune, we'll all be smitten
Embrace us, Death!

Come bombs and blow us all away
Our wide screens sets and cars of play,
Our latest diet and keep fit place
Fast food, canned breath.

Mess up the mess you've made of the town
A house for twenty thousand down
And never paid in fifty years
But never live to see!

And there the man whose life is veiled
Make sure the package is well nailed
Then let him wash away the sin
In women's tears.

It's not their fault – they do not know
The suffering on TV and radio
Go to a wedding so far away
Over in Nofaultistan.

Talk of things in trains and cars,
In dingy cafes and fast food bars –
But never look up and see the stars
Over in Nofaultistan.

Come evil bombs and fall on Britain
It can't be changed – it has been written
The cabbages are with us now
The Earth breathes out.

The Legend of the Corryvreckan

A Scandinavian Prince, Breakan, fell in love with a Princess of the Island, whose father consented to the marriage, on condition that Breakan should show his skill and courage by anchoring his boat for three days and three nights in the whirlpool. Breakan accepted the challenge and returned to Norway, where he had three cables made... one of hemp, one of wool and one from maidens' hair. The women of Norway willingly cut off their hair and plaited the rope. It was believed that the purity and innocence of the maidens would give the rope strength to stand the strain.

A Scandinavian Prince named Breakan,
Fell in love, as princes are wont to do –
With a lovely lass from the island
And this bonny lass loved the prince too.
Her father was none too happy though:
This young suitor must prove his skill
Three days he must stay in the whirlpool
The maelstrom should test his will.
Young Breakan accepted the challenge
His love had made him blind
Surely somewhere in Norway
The answers he could find.
He must somehow get three cables
That will hold his boat secure.
The first two were of hemp and wool
But he had to find one more.
The third would be of maiden's hair –
But the maidens must be pure.
This rope would be the strongest
And would hold his boat for sure.
The maidens of Norway lined up
To give the Prince their hair –
Woven by the finest weavers
He set sail without a care.

Breakan anchored in the whirlpool
And the cables were made secure
Then the cables were unwound
And taken back to shore.

That first day the hemp rope parted
The maelstrom had started to fight
But the other two ropes still held
And he survived the night
On the second night the wool rope snapped
It just couldn't take the strain.
Again they hung on through the night
Through all the stress and pain.
All hope now was on maiden's hair
Surely this would hold them tight
But the whirlpool was now furious –
Alas this rope parted – our prince had lost his fight.
The boat was then sucked under
With Breakan and his crew.
No one could survive the maelstrom
The lass's father knew.
But the prince's dog had somehow survived
And the dog he was so brave
He dragged the body back to the lass
Who buried him in Kings Cave.

And there was a girl consumed with guilt
When she heard of the fateful day
She wasn't as pure as she made out
It was her hair that gave way.

Ockerlolly

Don't ask me what it means because I don't know. I do know that if you heard the call and didn't act quickly, you could be in deep and serious trouble.

Improvisation was the name of the game. First you had to find the remains of a pram. This was a device for pushing babies around in. By the time the pram was abandoned, it would have been through four or five generations, and about the only part that could be recognised was the undercarriage, that is – wheels and axles. These parts were, more times than not, buckled but that was of no import to eager hands and minds. Please bear in mind no tools were available for this operation – we didn't have any. The wheels and axles were removed from the old pram, and any repairs carried out.

Then the search started for a suitable piece of wood, this had to be strong enough to support at least two boys – sometimes more. These pieces of wood were not easy to come by – but perseverance usually paid off. Engineering skills were then required to fasten the plank to the wheels and axles. The front axle had to be turnable of course to facilitate manoeuvrability. The hole through the plank was made by the ingenious method of borrowing a coal poker from the house, lighting a fire (very easy for young engineers even without matches), heating the poker to a very high degree, and forcing it through the plank at the appropriate point. We always achieved a super symmetrical hole. With the undercarriage in place, the only remaining part was the rope, or strong twine to enable the driver to steer. (The steering circle was only very small because the wheels would come in contact with the plank). This was usually obtained from the greengrocers. Although the shops were always devoid of anything to do with green groceries, they could always find a length of suitable material. With the project complete, there was no shortage of volunteers to be the test pilot.

A suitable street was chosen, usually the longest and steepest. The 'Bogey' was then launched. It was amazing how quickly warp speed was reached, and not long before the magic word 'Ockerlolly' was shouted out by the pilot. Everyone knew the word, milkman, paper man, dustman, doctor and all knew how to react. The only thing the Bogey didn't have was a brake! Bogies of course were all-year-round machines, but they always gave way to the seasonal games, which were eagerly awaited.

Winter games usually involved some physical activity to try to keep warm. We seemed to have long hard winters in my young days. This meant that the park lakes were usually frozen. We had incredible slides, and we were experts; a good slide could take you a hundred yards – our sense of balance was incredible. Sledging was great fun (there always seemed to be snow) and a good run of maybe four hundred yards would ensure you were well heated up by the time you had pulled your sledge back to the top. By the way, the sledges were all homemade and all different colours, which depending on what piece of old wood had been acquired for the project. I swear they were faster than any of the professional jobs that are on sale now.

Winter gave way to spring and this brought the much-awaited 'Whip and Top' season. All children loved whip and top. I can remember clearly the different kinds of tops. The very fat ones that were not very mobile, but allowed you to make lovely patterns on the large area with chalk (we used to pinch this from school). Then there was the ordinary top; this was smaller and good for manoeuvrability and patterns. Then there was the piece de resistance, the window smasher – yes that's what it was called. The window smasher had a very small stem and a flat top to it. This device was every child's dream. The window smasher apart from smashing windows – could spin in any situation, it could even climb up a wall spin horizontally then climb down the wall and still be spinning furiously. The sticks we used to drive these tops were about twelve inches long and had strips of leather thong about twelve to fifteen inches long attached, it was this thong striking the top which produced the spin. These whips could not be allowed today of course far too dangerous. I can never remember any accidents. You only had to hit yourself once – you never did it again.

Spring gave way to summer, which brought tennis and cricket. Tennis was another game which tested our manufacturing skills. Again a bit of wood was required and somehow this was whittled with an old pair of household scissors to roughly resemble the shape of a racket (mostly nothing like). The court was a gable end of a house, always a reliable opponent; I often wonder how we would have got on if we had had the correct gear and tennis courts. Cricket was very similar: a bat roughly shaped and wickets, again very rough and wickets wedged into another block of wood to keep them erect. Jack Hobbs and Larwood would have been proud of us. These games gave us hours of fun also.

Autumn brought Conkers. This was a serious business. Conkers were in turn roasted, boiled in vinegar and I have no doubt had many other applications applied to harden them for the matches. Some turned out like rock, and were literally unbreakable – well we thought they were – but someone always had one just a little harder. It was always sad when the last conker and winner was declared; we knew then we had a whole year to wait for the next season. Years in those days were a very long time.

I think I was the first person in the world to have inline skates. If we had had a successful morning collecting jam–jars (These would make a halfpenny for a pound jar, and a full penny for a two-pound jar) we could go to the rollerdrome for an hour. This was great fun, and we always returned bruised and battered. I had this idea to make my own skates and save myself some dosh. I found some old castors (can't remember where) and obtained two pieces of wood roughly the size of my feet. I then somehow fastened the castors in line two to each piece of wood. Unfortunately without any tools and the proper means of support they were not too successful. If only I had known about patenting ideas: all the kids have these now and not much different to my original ones of sixty years before.

We played skipping, lots of different games – the girls were by far the best at this though. But it kept us incredibly fit and slim, and we were with the girls. We played Taws. I loved taws (Marbles). There were quite a few different games; I liked one-called Jinx the best. Anyone remember Jinx? English taws were quite good especially after the war ended, but American taws were such lovely colours, they were in great demand but too expensive for most boys. We seldom had any cash. We Played Piggy – again pieces of wood were required. The piggy, about six inches long, was shaped at each end so it was off the ground. You then hit the end of the piggy – it flew in the air if you got it right, then whilst in the air you walloped it with your stick. The farthest hit was the winner. Not to be played where there were windows.

We played 'Hot rice'. We made a circle with legs apart and a ball was dropped in the centre. If the ball went through your legs, you were 'It'. The others ran away for a few seconds then 'It' had to throw the ball at the other players trying to hit their legs. It may sound silly but it was great fun.

My first bike was a collection of bits and pieces from old abandoned wrecks. How on earth I ever made it go I will never know. I can remember clearly our evening rides in the summer out into the surrounded fields and countryside; wonderful days. We used to play dare in the woods – I remember dangling from branches of trees hundreds of feet in the air (well, that's what it seemed like at the time) and being dared to drop. There was the inevitable broken leg or arm – but not one of mine, I escaped somehow.

With war very much in mind we decided to make guns. We never really realised just how successful we were. Again we had no tools, only rusted scissors and the odd blunt knife, and only wood to work with. When the stock of the pistol had been fashioned, we worked on the handle. The handle was carefully crafted to fit snugly to the stock. Strong elastic bands, which we somehow acquired, were then used to bind the handle to the stock. It took all a young boys strength to squeeze the handle a smidgen from the stock with one hand. Another very powerful band was attached to the front of the stock. The bullet (in our case a screw or nail) was inserted between the stock and the handle. The band from the front of the stock was then pulled back hard and slipped over the nail or screw. Because of the tension of the Stock/handle binding, the missile stayed put, although very much primed. I must tell you that although we were young we knew this weapon was potentially lethal and even at our tender years we had rules. No boy was ever allowed in front of a primed gun. This was good reasoning, because when pressure was applied to the handle the screw or nail took off with deadly accuracy and could penetrate a can or stick into a door at ten yards. We had hours of fun with these deadly weapons without any injuries.

It seemed to me that I was still a child when the buff envelope dropped through our letterbox. This letter was telling me to report for military service. In a very short time I graduated from home made elastic powered nail gun, to rifles and machine guns.

My childhood definitely ended at this point.

This Thing in Front

This thing in front is following me
It's weird I know but true
I've tried so hard to shake it off,
But it sticks to me like glue.

How can it follow from the front?
There's no sense in that I know
But this thing is trailing from the front
On whatever route I go.

This thing in front is following, and
I'm trying to break free
It's impossible to shear the link;
Why has it picked on me?

Whenever I look forward
I can always see this glow –
This thing in front is always there,
I can feel the dread, the woe.

Sometimes it even turns around
And mouths out words to me,
I always try to hear the words;
But there is no sound – you see.

This thing in front is following me
I think I'll lose my mind
You probably think the same as me!
Why isn't it behind?

Dante's Gate

Son taken from father
Daughter taken from mother
Brother taken from sister
Family destroyed like many other.

Not too far really
But might as well be a million miles away.
There is no way back
For child, adult, doctor or lawyer.

Provision brought over to sustain life
And left at fortress door
No chains or bars but no escape
The only life is a new one.

Marriage is allowed – but any child
Is removed immediately never to be
Seen again, agony on agony –
In this endless pain, both physical and mental.

Dante's gate is the point of entry with no return
For these pitiful creatures, and is aptly named.
As they are directed through the dark tunnel,
All hope is abandoned.

The invincible German army, hell bent
On world domination, stopped three hundred
Yards short of hell. This is their bridge too far.
No occupation here – their courage lost.

What is the crime that warrants such
Inhuman treatment? No crime at all
Just the misfortune to have the awful tag of
Leper attached to you.

The island place which housed those wretched souls
Living in these isolated conditions until the late fifties.
Holds lepers no longer –
But its name will live forever
The island of Spinalonga.

A Very Greek Wedding

The invitation

The lovely card arrived in January and invited my wife and I to a wedding in Crete. It said 'Please share in celebrating our love and happiness in Kalives, followed by much feasting and dancing by the beach'. With the invitation came a list of possible places to stay, and a list of possible flights and times. The couple had met in Kalives in northern Crete, and decided it would be nice to return there for their wedding.

A holiday in Crete seemed a great idea, and a wedding thrown in! Well it sounded too good to miss. We accepted the invitation and I e-mailed the contact we had been given in Kalives and booked a nice-sounding place. We had no problem booking a flight on the Internet, and so in January we were all set for our holiday in Crete, which was to be on Friday 2nd Sept 2005 at 7.30 pm. We had a long time to wait.

The journey

We had booked extra legroom on the Airbus 300 out of Manchester and had a most comfortable flight. A lovely meal of spicy chicken was enjoyed, and a nice bottle of wine supplemented the chicken. For entertainment Shirley was listening to a talking book, and I did a couple of crosswords and some 'Sudoku's. The four-hour flight seemed to pass very quickly, and we soon found ourselves descending into Chania Airport. Clearing the formalities and headed outside in to the glorious sunshine, we found our pre-booked taxi waiting for us.

Neither my wife nor I had been to Crete before and we were soon enjoying the half-hour ride to our villa. The route took us on a coast road in an easterly direction and it wasn't long after we left the airport before we started to see some magnificent scenery. We kept getting a glimpse of a glorious mountain range in land, which we now know were the 'White Mountains'. On our left was the vast expanse of Souda Bay. We had to drive all the way round the bay and the views were, superb. We did not at this time realise the significance of this amazing bay, nor did we know the significance of the large cemetery full of white crosses, which we kept glimpsing on the shoreline.

To say the taxi driver was completely mad would have been an understatement – he just did not like anyone in front of him. Double white lines and bad bends held no fear whatsoever for this guy. I was relieved to know we were in a Toyota – at least they have decent brakes. Some thirty minutes later we arrived at the outskirts of Kalives. The driver took three left turns into different properties, reversing out again in each case, before he finally announced we had arrived.

This should have been the 'Villa Petros'. There were no signs telling us that it was, so we had our doubts. We paid the twenty-five euros and gave him a 10 percent tip – only because we were relieved to get there in one piece. Walking into the enclosed garden was like entering paradise: it was covered with the most delightful flowers and shrubs. We looked for someone to greet us. Alas no one was about. I tried the door to the villa – it was open. It seemed like the one that we had booked so we entered and took our cases in. The place was spotless and the air conditioning was buzzing away, obviously awaiting guests – so we assumed we were those guests. Looking in the fridge we found bottled water and various other drinks, so being extremely thirsty we helped ourselves. On opening the patio doors a most amazing scene confronted us. The front of the villa looked directly onto Souda Bay, and the Mediterranean was lapping at our patio wall. I could have jumped from the patio into the warm waters of the Cretan Sea. This place was indeed a paradise. We unpacked and showered, found a taverna about two hundred yards away and had a lovely meal of pepper steaks and delicious ice cream. Oh yes, and a litre of very acceptable wine.

The next morning we still didn't know if we were in the correct place, having had no contact of any kind. After breakfast we walked the five or six hundred meters to the charming Cretan town of Kalives. Finding the small hotel where we knew some of the other wedding guests were staying, I did some more investigating and found the guy who I had made the villa booking with. It was a relief to know we were indeed in the correct place. Iannis, as he was called, had been tied up with other guests and assumed we would be okay. So far so good ...

Two interesting people

We returned to our villa to lie out in the sun amongst the beautiful flowers of the gardens and listen to the waves rolling in. Whilst lying there still unable to believe our good fortune at being here, an elderly gentleman appeared. He introduced himself as Pappa Petros Iannis. He was in fact the guy who had built this villa, and was of course the father of Iannis. After telling him what a super place it was and asking him a few questions about Crete I asked him if he remembered the German occupation. He did, and in fact he had been a member of the Partisans resistance movement.

He remembered the German paratroopers landing on Crete. He remembered the under-equipped, battle fatigued and under-trained allied troops who fought gallantly to hold Crete, but who had to be evacuated, Dunkirk-style to Egypt. The elite German troops managed to capture an airfield and then were able to land heavy equipment. They had vastly superior fire-power and also many aircraft (mostly bombers) overhead. The British navy took a terrible pounding in Souda Bay but apparently did a superb job getting many troops away. Retribution by the Germans was swift on those Cretans who helped the troops evacuate.

Many massacres, it seems, took place all over Crete. He told me that there is still one village with just old ladies living there. All their males were shot by the Germans.

The partisans did an incredible job harassing the enemy with hit and run tactics, with the help of small bands of allied specialist troops who were dropped in, and the Germans took many casualties. The cemetery we noticed on our way here was the one for the allied troops who were killed in the evacuation. It seems that Allied casualties in the campaign were about 17,500 killed, wounded, and prisoners; German losses, just over 6,000. In addition, 9 British warships were sunk, and 17 were damaged. After our talk Pappa Petros Iannis got on with his job of watering the gardens.

From our patio I could see most of Souda Bay, and it was not difficult for me to envisage the scenes just described to me by Pappa. Maybe this was because there is a large NATO base in the bay and war ships of various nations could be clearly seen sailing in and out of the bay, including nuclear submarines.

The next day Shirley and I were looking around the old village of Kalives and we got into conversation with an elderly Cretan gentleman. He spoke excellent English. He had just sold his house in Florida, and now shared his time between his London home and an apartment in Crete. I found out that he was a good friend of Pappa Iannis. He then told me that he was the commanding officer of the naval NATO base in Souda Bay until he retired. He was the most unassuming gentleman. I told him I had been in the Royal Air Force, and although he outranked me by a mile we had a very interesting conversation. He was a genuinely nice guy.

The wedding

Well the day had finally arrived. Shirley and I were to be picked up outside our villa at five-thirty. We had decided to give ourselves plenty of time to get ready. We had spent the day sunbathing and swimming in the warm sea. Then the bomb dropped! Shirley's watch was her late mother's gold analogue watch and she (Shirley) had omitted to wind it up. We had both fallen asleep, Shirley woke up and looked at the watch – it said three. The watch had stopped. It was in fact just turned five. Panic, panic. Although I tried to keep things calm it didn't work. What with hair and makeup and dresses and feminine things – would we be ready? We just made it in time. In fact we were okay, the coach which was conveying the guests was a little late. But we were sweating a bit. It was only on the coach that we found out the venue for the wedding. It was a place called Aptera. The wedding would actually take place in an old fort. Aptera dates back to the 6th century BC. The fort stands on a hilltop 230m high and has panoramic views over the plain of Chania and the Bay of Souda. It was easy to realise the significance of the fort with its dominating position. The fort could be Turkish or Roman origin but it certainly was very old. The views from the top were wonderful, we could now see the 'White Mountains' in all their glory, and the view of Souda Bay from here was amazing.

A room in the old fort had been prepared for the wedding. There were no facilities (water or electric) and the sound system was battery operated. A wedding coordinator had been hired and this lady would act as translator. The ancient stone room had been decorated with white lace droops, and candles were burning in every possible place. It really did look lovely. The mayor of Kalives was performing the civil ceremony, and then various friends contributed other readings. A hymn was sung and there was a short religious ceremony – exchanging rings etc. After the ceremony, crates of refrigerated Champagne were opened – and enjoyed.

We must have been at Aptera for two hours but it seemed to go very fast. I got some decent still and video shots. A photographer had been flown out from England to do the professional stuff. We were then coached back down to Kalives to the reception. We started off here with more Champagne, and then the feasting. I suppose we had a typical Grecian wedding feast. There were about six courses, the main meat seemed to be lamb. I remember having a spinach thingy. I don't like spinach, but this was delicious. There was anything one wanted to drink also.

The usual speeches and toasts followed, and then a professional Greek dancing troop arrived to entertain us. After their display, which was excellent, they instructed the guests in the steps to 'Zorba the Greek' and in a very short time the guests were snaking out over the sand all linked together, this was quite an amazing sight. More dancing, drinking and laughter later, the sky erupted with a magnificent firework display.

At about two of the clock on Saturday morning Shirley and I left the proceedings. We walked back to our villa through the now-deserted streets. Sitting on our patio a little later drinking a nice cup of coffee, we turned the sea light on, and this illuminated the breakers which where gently rolling in, a real fairy-land scene. We didn't say much. I am sure my wife was still thinking about the wedding, but I was looking across the bay to the twinkling lights on the distant peninsular and thinking about the carnage that had occurred in this bay not so many years ago ….

We had truly been to 'A Very Greek Wedding'.

Sadie's Story

The old shed came as a welcome sight,
It meant shelter from the cold in the coming night.
Just a small hole that she could squeeze through,
Then a long sigh as she thought 'This will do'.

She was weary and tired and lay down her head,
She needed to rest before making her bed.
In a few minutes she had sniffed all around,
But a few oily rags were all that she found.

This night would be the hardest, she knew that was true,
With no one to help, or show what to do.
Then with a shudder and a look so forlorn
She waited alone for her pups to be born.

In the slow growing light our very proud mum
Looked down in amazement at what she had done.
Seven lovely pups with eyes closed so tight,
And she'd managed alone in the dark of the night.

With seven weeks of scrounging and begging for food
She somehow kept healthy along with her brood,
The pups were now bigger and making more sound
And so as expected, at last they were found.

With the best of intentions they were taken to town,
Where the man in the cap said, 'Seven days then put down.'

But someone had heard of the poor family's plight,
'They will not be put down, that cannot be right –
They deserve much more, after what they've been through'
So straight down to town, to see what to do.

Now things turned out well for our caring mum,
She is warm and contented with food in her tum.
But there are seven little pups that need love and care,
Have you a nice house, and a heart you can share?

When the story made the paper and the pups' photos too,
The phone started ringing, and rang all day through.
With the applicants vetted, and selection all done
The pups said a final goodbye to their mum.

With bellies all bulging, coats shining like new
She knew she had done the best she could do,
So tired and thin, battle scars on her face,
She had raised them all well, without any disgrace.

She watched them all go with a whimper and groan,
And looking around found herself all alone.
With big brown eyes wide, she looked with a plea.
'They all wanted my pups, but no one wants me'.

Now Shep was eleven, and had just lost an eye,
But with all the pleading they'd give it a try.
He had always been spoiled, and would be number one.
With that understanding they said she could come.

The seven-mile journey took her to that place
Where in the large kitchen they met face to face.
They got on so well when they met the first day,
And if she behaved, they agreed she could stay.

With lots of good food, grooming and care,
Large gardens to play in and Shep's company to share.
She is thickening out, with coat gleaming bright,
We think that she knows everything is alright.

A trip to the vet, for a cut on the tum,
No more did they want their new friend to be mum.
And being experienced in matters of health
She even removed all the stitches herself.

Well this little verse brings you right up to date,
Oh! She's just started training – gosh what a state.
And if ever you meet our very proud lady
Stop and give her a pat, we've christened her 'Sadie'

A Purple Skeleton

Try rhyming a word with *diamond*?
You will be lucky if you do –
Okay now try *silver* and *orange*,
I think they're impossible too.
You may care to try with *nothing*,
But you won't get far I'm sure.
Or trying to rhyme something with *month*,
Will have you racking your brain some more.
You could of course try *skeleton*,
That's a funny one it's true.
You may just find you're *limited*,
But it gives the brain something to do.
Now have a try rhyming with *ninth*,
You will find that's a word too far.
What a beautiful colour is *purple*
But trying to rhyme it's a bar.
Now here is the real funny part,
Which word do you think is the best?
I'm putting my money on *poem* –
Cos' it's harder to rhyme than the rest….

PS. I'm off for a *pint* now,
Whoops there's another.

Scamp Writes to Australia

Dear Denmark,

My warmest canine salutation to you. My name is Scamp and unknown to my dad I read the e-mail that your dad sent. I pricked my ears up when I read the bit about you being a digger.

Well, let me tell you my friend, I am a multi-talented dog, but digging happens to be one of my greatest talents. My mum and dad recently moved house, they said it was because the gardens were too big. Well, I have to admit I was getting a little tired keeping them in order, you would have been proud of some of my achievements though. It really was good of them to move for me. The gardens now are much smaller and much easier for me to maintain, although sometimes they shout at me for not digging deep enough! I think they forget that I am nearly fourteen and only small.

I had a real corker the other day, I went out with the intention of really going for it – you know the feeling had a good dinner, emptied the bowels, had a good kip, preferably on the bed, or sun lounger. Had a few biscuits and then went for a good dig. Well, I don't know what happened but everything seemed to flow and go just right. I don't know about you Denmark but I use four paw drive (only amateur dogs use two) well I got going and it was amazing I have never been so deep, the soil just seemed to throw itself out of the hole.

My mum obviously wanted a big hole because she didn't interfere, usually she comes out, and if the hole is big enough, she stops me, but this day she didn't. I must have lost track of time (which is most unusual for me) because the next thing I remember my dad must have come home from work, and because I normally go to meet him, they were looking for me in the garden. One of my best digging areas is behind the garden shed. I can usually work undisturbed there.

And that was where they eventually found me. The problem was that I had disappeared from view. I had gone so deep that I couldn't get out. My dad had to lie down and reach into the hole and he just managed to get me out, unfortunately while pulling me out he fell in. Well, they must have been delighted with the hole because they both started laughing (that means they are happy). Unfortunately they must still think I can do better, because my dad said, 'If he had gone any further, he would have been in bloody Australia.'

Well now I am sure you will be getting the gist of this letter, it occurs to me, that if you are as good as your dad says you are, then maybe if you dig down, and I dig down, we could meet in the middle – or even have exchange visits. Anyway think about it and let me know if you are up to it. If you want any tuition to improve your action I would be pleased to help with a correspondence course.

My dad has just got a new car, it has air conditioning, and comfy seats. He knows I like to travel in style. I sit in the back and he drives me around. He is just like a dog with a new bone.

Well, I have to go now (I feel a dig coming on).

With lots of smells, licks and wags.
Scamp, M.R.C.D Oxon

PS JCB recently offered me a job, but I am just too busy to take it!

Good Friday in Los Gigantas

Fish leaping in the harbour
Boats bobbing to and fro
Music from every corner
People everywhere we go.

A million stars shine brightly
Sun's rays now on different land
Cliffs close their eyes and slumber –
As the sea retakes the sand.

Good Friday service in full swing
Church doors open wide –
Respectful silence around the church
As the faithful pray inside.

Then a miracle seems to happen
The moon appears so bright
And lights the mighty Teide –
So vast, so tall, so white.

Eine Gnadige Frau mit Vielem Wind

(Name that Tune)

This is about a German lady who suffered from the most appalling wind. This lady was able to turn her affliction into the most amazing art form, which earned her my total and lasting respect.

The golden sand, the hot sunshine
The sparkling sea, everything so fine.
Clothes all off, towels laid –
Worth every penny of what we paid.

A lovely beach with plenty there
But lots of room for us to share –
Then a rather large lady came sat by me,
And gazed out longingly to the sea.

I heard a tune, I knew it well
'Twas that famous canon by Pachelbel.
I looked around to find the source –
A radio it would be, of course?

But I soon realised that I was wrong!
When I heard the sound of another song.
No radio the cause I fear –
'Twas coming from the ladies rear.

Then the lady placed her hands down
And raised up from the sand.
The noise that was produced then –
Would be well described as grand.

The staccato that erupted
Really made us smile –
It was like a bloody broadside
From the Battle of the Nile.

She then moved on to Beethoven
And whilst we sipped some tea,
She played *Ode to Joy* from the *Choral*,
And the start of his *Fifth in C*.

This lady was an artiste true
A musician in every way,
She had a full four-octave range
And I'm sure could have played all day.

Now the lady favoured Wagner
And how could that be wrong?
We had a blast from *Tannhauser*
That came through loud and strong.

She even knew her *Lohengrin*
And coaxed it so discreet.
Her version of the wedding march
Came through so soft and sweet.

The lady looked with gratitude,
Her only aim, to please –
Then she raised her rear so slightly,
And gave us *Fur Elise*.

We played a game of 'name that tune'
And were nearly always right
Her pitch and tone so accurate
And her quality firm and bright.

Reluctantly we had to leave
This most unusual show,
We had to bathe and change our clothes
And so we had to go.

When we got back into our room
We lost control for sure,
And for a good half hour
We were rolling on the floor.

At last composed, bathed and changed
We headed late for dinner,
There was only just one table left
So I knew we were on a winner.

But I had been too confident
Of our safety I was wrong –
Our German lady was on the next table,
And the recital I knew would go on.

I hoped she could control herself
As we sat down and dined,
But she had a captive audience now
And was of a different mind.

It was just has I had finished soup
When I heard this splendid tune.
With a sheepish grin upon her face
She eased out *Claire de Lune*.

She entertained throughout the meal
Her repertoire was vast,
She even knew her Smetana –
And did *Vlatava* from *Ma Vlast*.

We finished our carafe of wine
To the sound of a Schubert *Lieder*
And made our exit from the room
To the Grand March from *Aida*

We will never forget that lady
And soon find ourselves in tears,
Our memory of her will never fade
And will stay for all our years.

Le Petomane*, had nothing on her,
The control of notes was so pure –
No matter where the sound came from,
One had to yearn for more.

I wonder what she will make of life?
Surely fortune will be in her reach.
Or will she be content with her life as it is?
With her free daily shows on the beach.

The lady has such talent; she really could go far,
If she gets herself a manager she could surely be a star.
Or if she gets some medical help and her problem goes away,
My wife and I feel privileged we were there to hear her play.

Le Petomane. One Joseph Pujol, a Frenchman had a similar ability. He performed his act at the Moulin Rouge between 1887 to 1914. A film was made starring Leonard Rossiter in 1979.

And the Earth Moved

I will start at the beginning, which was 2.30am, and the alarm clock was sounding.

Shirley and I were to be at the airport for 3.15. We both thought this a little silly and aimed for 3.45, as it turned out the high security alert had been eased a little and we had plenty of time. The aircraft took off on time at 6.15 am. Our destination was Zante, an island off the West Coast of Greece in the Ionian Sea. (Also known as Zakynthos).

The aircraft quickly gained speed down the runway and I became aware of a vibration that just did not seem right. Just after takeoff the vibration stopped. I did not want to alarm my wife, so I remained quiet. After about fifteen minutes the pilot came on the intercom. The vibration was from the front landing gear. The pilot had been in touch with the relevant authorities and because there was no engineering facility available on Zante, it was decided to return to the airport. We were assured everything would be okay and all the emergency services had been alerted. We were expected back in fifteen minutes. Until we were actually on the ground there were some very frightened people on that plane. We were then informed that because the plane would have to be jacked up to be worked on, all passengers would have to leave, and all baggage be removed. We lost two hours, and some passengers were reluctant to reboard the plane. Eventually we took off again and all seemed okay. The rest of the flight was uneventful and we landed without any problems.

Our hotel was not far from the airport and our waiting taxi soon had us there. We quickly changed and unpacked and shortly afterwards were walking on a delightful beach in wonderful warm sunshine. The beach we were on was Kalamaki, this is a designated protected site for the under threat Loggerhead turtles. The nests are clearly marked and the beach is closed each day from seven in the evening to seven in the morning for the young to make their way from egg to sea. Normal activity takes place on the beach through the day but many restrictions are in place. No motor boats, no fishing, no light of any kind after dark, no interfering with nests etc. It is all very interesting, but the young people who have volunteered to protect these delightful creatures are very short of funds. My daughter, who is a teacher, has got her school children interested and they are doing a project and starting to raise funds to help the survival of the turtles, these creatures have many predators and need all the help they can get to make it to adults

After showering and changing we found a nice looking taverna about fifteen minutes walk from out hotel. We were warmly greeted by the staff and ordered a carafe of wine whilst we perused the menu. The wine arrived, but before we could pour any out, the whole place started to shake. In the background was a very loud rumbling noise. We were in fact having an earthquake. It seemed to last for about a minute but in reality it was probably about fifteen or twenty seconds. But scary it certainly was. The staff tried to reassure their customers, but it was clear that they were a little worried too. We had an enjoyable meal and made it back to the hotel without any problems. The next day the hotel manager told us that the report he received stated the tremor was five on the Richter scale. That was a fair old rumble we had experienced, and it was the first topic of discussion whilst we were there.

Now do you think you could get through a whole week with your watch one hour out? Well Shirley and I did just that. On arrival the time was given out by the crew as being one hour in front of ours. I argued that it should be two hours, but was shouted down by people who seemed to know, so our watches were put forward one hour. Through the week things happened that made us think something was wrong. When I went for early morning run lots of people were about, normally the beach is deserted at seven am. The morning mail plane which was scheduled for seven am each day, always flew over us at six and woke us up.

When we went for our evening meal early, no later than seven, everyone else had also decided to go at seven. We truly never twigged what was wrong until the last day. I had an hour to spare, as our taxi was due at 10am, so I took myself off to the beach for a last look around and a few last minute photo shots. Strolling slowly back, watching the lizards stretching in the morning sun, my wife suddenly appeared on the scene – the taxi had arrived. She had argued with reception that the taxi was in fact an hour too early. Our watches of course told us it was only nine. The truth slowly dawned on us; we had been running an hour slow for a week and didn't realise it – what a pair of plonkers! We had to bribe the taxi driver to hang about while we finished packing; he was okay about it. Don't think it could never happen to you either (it just may do at sometime).

As can be expected these days, the plane was held up by a so-called computer fault at its departure point and was an hour late arriving at Zante. That meant another hour wait at the airport; we were not amused. The aircraft eventually loaded and headed for the runway. Our attempted take off was soon aborted though. A forest fire had started some distance away and two water tanker aircraft had somehow been given priority clearance on our runway (you couldn't make this up). That meant another half-hour delay. Well, we got off eventually and knew of course that nothing else could go wrong. Nothing did until we were nearly on the ground, four hours later. The wheels were down the flaps were set and the ground looked only feet below us when – full power was applied and the plane literally stood on its tail and went vertical. The undercarriage was raised and off we went soaring into the heavens. I can assure you everyone on the plane was frightened. After about five minutes the captain voice came over the intercom. He had to abort the landing as there was a helicopter very near to the runway – yes you read that correctly. We went round again and lost another half-hour at least. It was wonderful to feel solid ground under our feet once more. Our cases were of course the last on the carousel – as usual.

My car had survived its stay at the airport car park without any problems, and we were soon on our way home down the motorway.

Don't these little things just add a little ambience to one's life?

Graduation

Tell me about the whale, the tiger and the bear;
Tell me about foxes, the tortoise and the hare.
Tell me about the mountains, of woodland, and the snow;
Tell me about the rains, and the winds that used to blow.
Tell me about children, and warm days in the sun;
Tell me about laughter, playing games and fun.
Tell me about feelings, of anger and despair;
Tell me about sadness, happiness and care.
I know these things are written down,
But can I believe the pen
They say that you once went there –
Were there really things called men?

Oliver Twist

This poem is in the form of 'rime royal' which is ten syllables per line, and seven lines per stanza. It has five stanzas, with rhyming pattern of ababbcc. It has also been written as a 'shrinklet,' which is a compressed version of a famous story.

Poor Oliver in a workhouse was born,
The lad never knew his unhappy mum.
He arrived in the middle of a storm
And he would grow to hate, where he had come;
There was never enough food in his tum,
He asked for more, but was outdone you see
And so was sold on in his misery.

He just did not like working with the dead
And planned to run away, if he could.
To eat, they would gave him gruel and bread,
They thrashed him, hit him, if still he stood.
In a coffin he slept, all made of wood.
A daring escape he made, and then lo,
To old London town, he set off to go.

He was met by the Dodger in tall hat,
Had Oliver anywhere for to stay?
He could soon feed him up, make him more fat.
And could find him a place that very same day.
Would he please now come without any delay?
Old Fagin and boys met him with wide grins;
Fagin showed Oliver his pretty things.

Bill took poor Oliver with him to steal;
This action made our poor Nancy see red.
The lad was thinking about his next meal,
Nancy feared that she could well end up dead;
Bill Sykes was so clearly out of his head,
He killed the poor girl, oh my what a shame
That was the end to Bill Sykes' little game.

Fagin then off to the prison did go
Bill Sykes was destined to take a big swing.
An old uncle said, that young man I know,
From a picture in a brooch on a string.
And together they all started to sing.
Oliver could now begin his new life
Now released from his shackles and strife.

Me and my Shadow

Just before my wife and I were due to go to Lanzarote in March, I became aware of a sharp pain in my left thigh. I was running about twenty miles a week at the time and cycling twice that amount. I thought I may have pulled a muscle, a common occurrence with runners, but I wasn't aware of having done so. I thought a visit to the doctor's may be prudent. After a good examination, he told me that a week in the sun would put things right, and I should go on holiday. We had booked seats on the plane with extra legroom, so I knew I would be reasonably comfortable on the flight of about four hours.

We were staying in a five star hotel and were given a lovely room with a southern facing large balcony, looking out to sea. I knew things were not right shortly after going to bed the first night. The pain that I had in my left thigh now started up in my right thigh, in exactly the same spot. I had a very uncomfortable night. The next morning I could hardly get out of bed, I was in so much pain. Eventually I loosened up enough to go down for breakfast.

During the week I gradually got worse, I couldn't sleep or even move in bed, I could not put my socks or shoes on myself. I lost my appetite. The pain that had started in one thigh was now in both legs and down into my lower legs. Common sense should have told me to contact a doctor, but having gone to my own doctor before the holiday, this problem was known about, and would have rendered my insurance void. The only redeeming thing was the spring sunshine. I was able to lie on the balcony and enjoy the warming rays. The flight back was very uncomfortable for me and it seemed endless. I was never so happy to see my own home.

The next morning I was at my doctor's first thing. It was a different doctor to the one I saw before the holiday. I explained my symptoms, he examined me, and wasn't sure what the problem was. I was dispatched to our local hospital for a blood test and was given a course of steroid tablets – fifteen mg per day. The blood test revealed all was not correct, but at this stage I didn't know why. After about three days I was getting worse and returned to the doctors. This time it was a lady doctor and once again I had to explain everything. She arranged for another blood test and increased my steroid dose to thirty mg per day.

I had started to investigate my problem on the internet by this time, and discovered I had the classic symptoms of polymyalgia. This is an inflammation of the blood vessels in the muscles. It is not known what triggers it, and there is no known cure. It can only be controlled by Prednisolone, the steroid drug I had been given. Polymyalgia usually starts in the shoulders and generally only affects women. No wonder the diagnosis was difficult. The thirty mg of Prednisolone stopped the pain dead. I felt great again. It was then that I started to take notice of the effects of the steroid. Prednisolone is a corticosteroid drug. These have potent anti-inflammatory properties, and are used in a wide variety of inflammatory conditions. The number of possible side effects are frightening, and in many cases people had to stay on high doses for up to four or five years. Over fifteen mg per day was considered to be dangerous territory.

By this time I had had a number of blood tests – still not right, and the doctors agreed that my problem was most probably polymyalgia. It was thought at this stage that I should see a specialist and an appointment was made. I had also started to reduce my intake of steroids. This had to be done carefully and also logged. I had to carry a card with me at all times detailing my steroid intake per day.

I had resumed some gentle jogging with the doctor's permission, and it was during one of these jogs that I became short of breath and had to stop. I walked home and rang the doctor immediately as I was quite alarmed. He told me to come to his surgery straight away. I was on his couch being examined within ten minutes. My steroid input was discussed and we agreed to go for a lower dose. I was also to have a chest X-ray and yet another blood test the next day. One week later I returned for the results. My blood sedimentation rate (SED) was still high and causing him some concern. Whilst I was there my chest X-ray result came through from the hospital. After a few moments he told me that there was a shadow on it.

I knew that the steroid treatment was zapping my white blood cells and although this was controlling the myalgia, it was leaving me wide open to any infection that I came into contact with. The white blood cells of course do our battles for us, taking care of viral and bacterial attacks. I suggested to the doctor that I may have picked up a bacterial infection, and this could be showing as consolidation on the X-ray. He was thinking the same way – and it was decided a large dose of antibiotics were required. One week later I returned for a second X-ray. The shadow was still there. My doctor rang the consultant and my appointment with him was brought forward two weeks.

On Friday morning the third of June I was due to fly to Corfu. The holiday was to celebrate our wedding anniversary and also our daughter's birthday.

On Thursday afternoon the consultant listened to my story and then started his tests. Whilst I was getting dressed he left the room and returned about ten minutes later. He told me he had been to talk to a colleague and he wanted me to have a CT scan the next week. I told him that I was due to go on holiday the next day to Corfu and I would be away for a week. He then told me that they thought I had a blood clot and that I should not fly. To be told I could not go was a disaster. I was not under any pressure from my wife or daughter, although they were disappointed, they understood the situation. It was my decision to go ahead with the holiday rightly or wrongly. I knew my private insurance would be void, and I would be relying totally on my E111 form.

At five am on Friday, our daughter picked Shirley and I up for the forty minute drive to Robin Hood airport, near Doncaster. At seven-thirty we were airborne and heading for Corfu. We were quite comfortable, having once again reserved seats with extra legroom. The flight was superb and we had excellent views of Holland, Germany, the Alps and Croatia. A hire car was waiting for us at the airport in Corfu, and we were soon on our way to Agios Stevanos on the north-west of the island. We arrived at our villa about forty minutes after leaving the airport. Although the roads are fairly good, some of the bends are horrendous and great care is required, local drivers seem to have very little regard for visitors, who have to drive much more slowly. The villa could only be described as superb. It was situated on a hillside overlooking a pretty village and harbour, with extended views over the channel to Albania. We had our own private swimming pool and olive and orange tree. We ate oranges straight from the tree and also used them to make drinks. Down in the village we could watch the comings and goings of various types of boats, by the size of some of the boats I think there was some rich people about. There were a number of tavernas by the harbour, and the food was excellent.

Corfu used to have a feral dog problem; this fortunately is now a thing of the past. We did see dogs but they were well fed and cared for. The problem now is feral cats.

These poor creatures are everywhere and although the problem is now being addressed it will clearly take a long time to achieve any success. I think we spent more money on feeding the cats than we did on our own food. It started with just one pregnant cat which visited our villa. It must have told its mates that it was being fed and watered because we soon had a queue. We started off by giving them cat food and milk, but they also had tuna and chicken. We left some happy cats behind us, and hoped that others would take over when we left. If these cats were rounded up and doctored then the problem would soon go away, at the moment the cats are just breeding machines. How can you ignore starving creatures?

So our lovely week in the Greek sunshine drew to an end and I had enjoyed a very relaxing holiday. We arrived back home on Saturday morning. My gamble had paid off.

From being on thirty mg of Prednisolone per day in March, I have managed to come down to two mg per day. I am feeling the effects of this low dose, but am determined to keep it as low as possible. I now have to go for my CT scan, and hopefully get this shadow and breathing problem sorted out. I am determined that I will be doing the three R's again before too long: Reading – 'Riting – and Running.

Pulmonary Embolism (PE) has a thirty-two percent mortality rate. Seventy-five percent will die within the first hour. It is not always easy to diagnose. I had classic symptoms: very severe pain in the groin and thigh of left leg. This eventually changed to my other leg. I had tachycardia (an uneven heartbeat) and I developed breathing problems. I was sent for an X-ray. This displayed a shadow in lower right lung. After antibiotics I had another X-ray this also displayed the shadow in lower right lung. I had repeated blood test. These were telling us something was wrong. Still I wasn't diagnosed. It took a doctor at the hospital, from a different discipline altogether, to suspect I had a PE. I requested a CT scan on my first visit to my GP. I actually had one 16 weeks later. It was found that I had an embolism blockage, in my right lung.

In fairness I didn't present with many of the symptoms – out of a table of thirteen, I had four. But they were classic. I think it should have been picked up earlier. Many malpractice cases are brought as a result of failure to diagnose PE. But these are usually after death has occurred. Non-diagnosed PE cases cause more deaths per year than breast cancer.

Friday the 24th of June was the day of my Pulmonary Angiogram at York District Hospital. It also happened to be the day when numerous cars decided to crash on the A1 above Wetherby, effectively closing it to all northbound traffic. The consequence of this was that the traffic was being diverted via York towards Harrogate were it would rejoin the A1 near to Boroughbridge and so bypass the crashes. York was brought to a standstill and was gridlocked. Our intention was to set off at nine, park up, and then have a walk round York and a coffee, before a leisurely walk to the hospital for my appointment at noon. It would normally take no more than an hour to drive to York. At 11.15 we were on the outskirts of York but still stuck in unmoving traffic. I managed to negotiate some country lanes that I remembered from my teens, and approached the city from the east side, this was relatively traffic free, we arrived at the hospital with about two minutes to spare. The CT department was dealing with an emergency accident case so we were able to get our coffee and relax a little after all. I went into the CT room about 12.45.

For a pulmonary angiogram a cannula is inserted in the arm and connected to a high-pressure pump. When the CT scan starts, the pump is triggered and the medium is injected. The contrast medium travels to the lungs. There is no pain involved – but it is very uncomfortable. When the medium was injected I got a very hot feeling all over my body, and a very nasty metallic taste in my mouth. After about fifteen minutes the cannula was removed from my arm and I was allowed to go.

I was told my GP would be in touch in about ten days. We arrived home at about four; the traffic was still bad, but not in the direction we were going. At about four thirty we had a telephone call, my wife answered it. It was my consultant from the hospital. The CT scan had been viewed almost immediately, and had revealed a double pulmonary embolism – 'potentially lethal'. I was told to get to hospital as fast as possible. Fortunately my daughter was at hand to take me, and we were at the hospital very quickly.

On reporting to the acute admissions department, it was explained to me that I had a serious condition, and I was immediately put into bed. The action then started. I have to tell you here that I felt perfectly well. I was not displaying any outward signs of chest problems. Within a short time I had needles in everywhere – both taking things out, and putting things in. This activity lasted until about two-thirty in the morning.

I was then trundled down to the X-ray dept for another chest X-ray. When I offered to walk, I was told in no uncertain terms that I was not walking anywhere.

My later discussion with the medical staff centred on how I had come to have this pulmonary embolism; it should not have happened to me. I was not the right candidate: no family history; nothing in my past to tie it in; nothing in my lifestyle, diet, weight etc. I had been a lifetime athlete. It did not make sense. This it seems was why this condition had not been suspected. You will remember I had my first signs, a bad pain in my left thigh, in March. I suffered breathing problems about six weeks ago. Both classic signs of a potential PE – yet no one tied in the link or even suspected. A blood clot in the lungs is the most serious one you can have, and it very often fatal. I have indeed been very lucky, especially when the time span is considered and what I had done in that period. Everyone I had contact with in the hospital was superb. I had excellent care. The doctors and nurses were very friendly and willing to answer my many questions. My biggest praise though must go to the guy who diagnosed my PE. If it hadn't been for him I may not have been typing this. He was a Rheumatologist. My request to see a chest consultant was turned down. That guy deserves a knighthood.

I was allowed to go home from hospital but have had to return for Fragmin injections and blood tests each day. Fragmin is the drug which has an instant effect on reducing potential clotting of the blood. I am also taking Warfarin but this does not kick in for five days, so the blood has to be carefully monitored to bring you within the range required. This is the INR (International Normalised Ratio). For a normal person this is .8 to 1.2. My range has to be 2 to 3, considerably higher. I have just achieved 2 so I am now within range and can stop Fragmin and just rely on Warfarin. Fragmin injection are not nice, that are given in the stomach. I have still to have daily blood tests, these will now done at my own doctor's surgery.

This blood has to be sent to the hospital path labs each day, where my Warfarin dose is calculated; it is very important that it stays within range. The hospital then rings me with my dose rate. If the dose rate is wrong it can have fatal consequences. I have been told that the blood clot should start to dissolve itself. Surgery wasn't considered necessary, thank goodness and hopefully I should return to a normal lifestyle, which includes running again.

I will have to take the Warfarin for six months at least.

I am writing this in stages because I am not allowed to sit for more than a few minutes at a time. By the way – Warfarin does not thin the blood. This is a wrong conception. Warfarin acts on the Vitamin K content of the liver and reduces the clotting range of the blood slightly. The viscosity of the blood in a

normal person and one on Warfarin is exactly the same.
And that brings you up to date – lol.

PS This all happened in 2004, I have now resumed a normal lifestyle. The last respiratory consultant I saw told me that in her opinion my condition was caused by a hip injury I received in a nasty fall from my cycle, five months before my first symptoms. It is interesting to note that everyone concerned knew about this hip injury, and had seen the wound, but no one else thought it significant.

No Blandish for Miss Orchids

A Blandish was recently put up for sale on eBay. Offers rose in just 30 minutes to over four thousand pounds, before eBay were forced to withdraw it from sale. The Blandish is not legal in the UK at the present time. However it is thought that this decision is currently under discussion.

No Blandish for Miss Orchids,
These words just bring such pain.
No Blandish for Miss Orchids,
Does she just wait in vain?
Her friends have now all got one.
And they always bring such glee.
But no Blandish for Miss Orchids,
Why does this have to be?
She knows about the Blandish
The things that it can do –
The Blandish is so versatile
And does amazing things for you.
The girls don't come around much now,
Just too busy with their thing –
But Miss Orchids knows their progress,
And the wonders it can bring.
Miss Orchids was now desperate
Eyes never left her gate –
Friends won't share their Blandish.
She must bear the pain and wait.
But then the magic day arrived,
The postman she did spy –
Walking down her garden path,
With a twinkle in his eye.
Miss Orchids hand was shaking
As the form she tried to sign.
Then she gently took the box,
'At last, at last it's mine'.
She carefully unwrapped the box,
And the Blandish came in view.
She just sat down and stared at it,

Her prayers had all come true.
No more drugs or drinking –
No more men, or fear.
No more doubts or sorrow,
Her heaven is now here.
So Miss Orchids has her Blandish now,
It's resting in her hand.
Miss Orchids has her Blandish now,
Isn't life just grand?

Closing Down Sale

Snow, wind, hail, sunshine, rain,
Acid rain.
Wide sea, deep sea, stormy sea,
Dead sea.
Straight rivers, winding rivers,
Wide rivers, narrow rivers,
Deep rivers, shallow rivers,
Poisoned and dying rivers.
Birds, fish, insects, animals,
Sweet smelling ladies
With ivory jewellery,
And beautiful fur coats.
Plants, weeds, flowers, trees,
Our children won't need any of these.
Laser bombs
Suicide bombs
Soldiers – Terrorists
Small men, large men,
Dull men, bright men,
Silly men, clever men,
Scientists, politicians,
Salesmen, Super-salesmen,
Giant clear out,
Everything to go.

1936 (MCMXXXVI)

A very important year
Just a few things that made the headlines in 1936
Not in any particular order.
How much can you remember?

1936 was a leap year. It was also the year of the Olympic Games in Germany.

Italy claimed Ethiopia as their territory and invaded. With the economic situation worsening in Italy, Mussolini needed to take some action that would distract his people. The modern Italian army fought against Ethiopian tribesmen in Addis-Ababa.

The League of Nations censured Italy – but that was the extent of world reaction to the invasion.

Spain's civil war began in 1936 when nationalist troops under the command of General Franco rose up against the democratic republic.

The Arab rebellion against the British Government in Palestine, and opposition to Jewish immigration started – it lasted until 1939.

In violation of the treaty of Versailles, Nazi Germany reoccupied the Rhineland.

Bruno Hauptmann was convicted of kidnapping and killing Charles Lindbergh. He was executed in New Jersey the same year.

The first flight by Aer Lingus took place, and The Queen Mary left Southampton on her maiden voyage across the Atlantic.

The Hoover dam was completed in 1936 on the Colorado River in America. Construction began in 1931, and it was completed two years ahead of schedule In 1931 The Bureau of Reclamation opened bids for the construction of Boulder (Hoover) Dam and Power Plant. The contract was awarded to Six Companies; a construction and engineering firm made up of some of the West's most successful builders and designers of dams, bridges, roads, and tunnels. The winning bid was $48,890,995.

In November of 1931 The Colorado River was diverted around the dam site, and in 1933 the first concrete was poured in. In February 1935 water was released into the dam, and in May that year the last concrete was poured in.

In March 1947 a resolution was passed to change the name from Boulder Dam to Hoover Dam in tribute to President Hoover. President Truman signed the document and the name was changed. This project is still considered to be one of the greatest engineering feats of all time.

Al-Azhar 'Egyptian Muslim School', sent a large delegation to India to convert the untouchables there to Islam.

Oil was discovered in Saudi Arabia, making it the richest country on earth.

The last Tasmanian Tiger (Thylacine), a female, died alone in a cage in Hobart.

Walter Freeman performed the first frontal lobotomy in the United States

Music of 1936

>A fine romance.
>
>I'm putting all my eggs in one basket.
>
>Is it true what they say about Dixie?
>
>It's a sin to tell a lie.
>
>The music goes round and round.
>
>Pennies from heaven.
>
>There's a small hotel.
>
>These foolish things.
>
>The way you look tonight.

Great films of 1936

>'Things to come' Raymond Massey
>
>'Follow the Fleet' Fred Astaire. Ginger Rogers. Randolph Scott.
>
>'The Great Ziegfield' William Powell. Myrna Loy.
>
>'Modern Times' Charlie Chaplin. Paulette Goddard. (This is still considered to be one of the greatest films ever made).
>
>'Mr Deeds goes to Town'. Gary Cooper. Jean Arthur.
>
>'Romeo and Juliet' Moira Shearer. Leslie Howard.
>
>'Rose Marie'. Nelson Eddy. Jeanette Macdonald.
>
>'Swing Time'. Astair and Rogers again.
>
>'San Francisco'. Clarke Gable. (This film was the first big budget epic)

Film academy awards

    Best Film: 'The Great Ziegfield'

    Best Actor: Paul Muni in 'The Story of Louis Pasteur'

    Best Actress: Luise Rainer in 'The Great Ziegfield'

Nobel prizes for 1936

    The Prize for literature went by Eugene Gladstone O'Neill.

Victor F Hess shared the physics prize for his discovery of cosmic radiation, with Carl D Anderson for his discovery of the positron.

The prize for medicine went to Sir Henry H Dale and Otto Loewi for discoveries relating to transmission of nerve impulses. (England and Austria)

    Carlos Saavedra Lamas of Argentina won the Peace Prize.

Mercedes-Benz introduces the world's first production passenger car to operate on diesel fuel.

Ferdinand Porche introduced the Volkswagen 'peoples-car' in Germany.

Hienrich Foche also in Germany, developed the first practical helicopter the FA61.

Foche invented variable pitch, so his helicopter could fly backwards.

The last public execution took place in the USA in Kentucky. One Rainey Betha a black male of about twenty-six years was hanged. He admitted the rape and murder of a seventy years old white woman.

Sport

In boxing this was the year that Max Schmeling knocked out Joe Louis in the twelve round of their heavyweight match in New York. Louis later gained his revenge against Schmeling knocking him out in the first round of the re-match.

The 1936 summer Olympic games were held in Berlin, the German bid was preferred over Barcelona by the IOC in April 1931. The games were awarded before the Nazi Party came to power in Germany. These were the first games were the Olympic torch was carried by relay from Olympia. While Germany dominated the games, the many triumphs by other nations were seen as a rebuke to Nazi philosophies.

Anti-fascists in Barcelona planned to have their own games as an alternative games to Berlin in protest, but these games had to be cancelled because of the outbreak of the Spanish civil war. (It is interesting to note that the 1992 games in Barcelona were held in this same stadium). Germany came out top and led the field with 89 medals in the summer Olympics, America was second with 56. The UK won 14 medals.

These were the games where the great J.C. Owens (James Cleveland) Owens, better known – although wrongly, as Jessie Owens, had his major triumph. He won four gold medals and broke four world records. It is stated that Adolph Hitler would not acknowledge Owens, however Owens emphatically claimed that he [Owens] waved to Hitler and that he [Hitler] smiled at him and waved back, propaganda maybe? (A lot about at that time).

Owens developed a strong friendship with his strongest opponent in the long jump.

The German Carl Ludwig 'LUZ' Long. Owens owes his long jump success to Long who helped him with his take off, when he [Owens] had only one jump left to qualify.

Long placed his towel at the correct take off point for Owens, giving his own chance of winning away. Owens went on to win gold and stayed a firm friend with Long after the games. Long was presented with a special medal for sportsmanship. He was sadly later killed whilst serving in the German army in WW2. The American press also reported wildly on this unusual friendship between an American Black and a German white athlete.

These Games were the first to have television coverage; seventy hours of coverage were displayed on special screens throughout Berlin. It was not high - resolution television though, not being electronically scanned or transmitted.

The winter Olympics were held in Garmisch-Partenkirchen, Bavaria, and started on February the sixth. By coincidence that was where I first donned skis many years later. I have actually been on that same downhill Olympic course.

England launched the first high definition television service in the world.

America's experiments with 343-line television began from the Empire State Building.

The Crystal Palace was destroyed by fire. It was built in 1851 for the Great Exhibition.

Elstree film studios were also gutted by fire.

The Post office speaking clock (first in the world) was introduced in England.

King Edward V11 signs an instrument of abdication at Fort Belvedere.

Prince Albert 'Duke of York' becomes King.

Gatwick airport was opened.

Jarrow march. 200 unemployed miners marched from Jarrow on Tyne to London to present a petition to Downing Street. 80pc of people in the area were unemployed.
They were sustained on the march by donations from the public.

Gone with the Wind was published.

John Masefield was Poet Laureate in 1936.

To many, John Masefield is simply known as the poet who wrote about the sea. It is interesting to note that although Masefield's poems of sea and ships are well known, the poet himself in fact spent only a very small part of his life aboard ship. Sea life did in fact not suit Masefield and on his second voyage, he deserted ship to find work on land in New York. John Masefield also wrote novels and short stories, but it seems these are difficult to locate now. Below are some of his poems which you will no doubt remember from your schooldays. Who could forget 'Sea Fever' and 'Cargoes' and: A Ballad of John Silver, Christmas Eve at Sea, A Consecration, Trade Winds, The Wonderer, Spanish Waters, Roadways?

The YMCA was founded in New York.

Births in 1936 :-

Glen Campbell.

Roy Orbison.

Engelbert Humperdink. (pop singer)

Bobby Darin.

Yves Saint Laurent.

Robert Redford.

Buddy Holly.

Silvio Berlusconi.

62 – Gerald Finlay

Deaths in 1936 :-

> Rudyard Kipling.
>
> King George the fifth.
>
> G.K. Chesterton.
>
> Maxim Gorky.
>
> Louis Bleriot.

I hope you enjoyed this little tour of 1936, and apologies if I left anything out that you though should be mentioned – but 1936 was a very busy year.

Oh yes I did forget one very important birth – I made my appearance on July the eighth of that year. What an amazing year to be born.

Penance

'Has anyone heard people calling?'
The man in the black cape said –
'Has anyone seen people passing?'
As the hood blew back from his head.
He was tired and weary, chilled to the bone,
Torment had long passed him by –
He just wanted the chance for redemption,
As he once more called out with a sigh.
His mind went back many years before,
When he galloped this road to his love.
He knew what a-waited at the castle –
Her promise had heated his blood.
He remembered the Hag by the side of the cart,
Her scream for help as he sped by;
He remembered the young girl pinned 'neath the wheel
But more important things were nigh!
He remembered the chamber in the castle –
Where they lay side by side on the bed,
He knew he had just been to heaven;
The delight that was spinning his head.
Then the warmth disappeared just as fast as it came;
A cold dagger was thrust in his heart;
He leapt off the bed – he'd remembered,
The hag, and the girl 'neath the cart.
He sped down the road even faster this time,
His priority he knew had been wrong
He knew he should have stopped – to help,
'God – Why is it taking so long?'
At last the cart came into view, and –
He leaped from his horse with a thud,
Calling out loud to the hag and the girl;
Both now dead, 'neath the wheel, in the mud.
His penance then, was to stand by the road,
His memories ripping his heart;
To look for the hag, the cart, and the girl –
To try to get back to the start.
'Has anyone heard people calling?'
The man in the black cape said
 'Has anyone seen a cart and a girl?'
As the hood blew back from his head.

I Sold the World

I sold the World some days ago,
It wasn't worth a lot.
A bloke said how much is it?
I said 'give me what you've got.'
At first I tried to auction it
But it didn't reach reserve
The bidding stopped at fifty
And that's more than you deserve.
I remember when I made it
I was so pleased so proud
The best thing that I ever did
I shouted it out loud.
Have you ever thought what was involved
How much sweat and pain?
To present you with my perfect place
But alas it was in vain.
I tried to think of everything
To answer all your need
But nothing was quite good enough
You destroyed it all with greed.
When I think of all the animals
All the trees and flowers too
It never did occur to me
What destruction you would do.
I'm not bothered about you humans now
With your hate and need for power
I'll be glad to see the back of you
But please leave me just one flower.
Yes it's too late now; I've done the deed
The Earth's no longer mine
And that's a mighty burden lifted
Yes – I actually feel fine.
Now I'm going off to pastures green
I have a place to view
But this time it will be okay
Not like when I trusted you.

Now about the Earth's new owner
I'm sure you'd like to know.
You lot will like him very much
I'm sure on you he'll grow.

But nothing's ever free you know
You'll have a price to pay
And this guy comes expensive
Exorbitant I'd say.
So when he comes for payment
And you cannot pay his bill
Don't bother trying to call on me
And I know for sure you will –
Well how much did I get for it?
I can hear some of you say,
In the end I couldn't take it –
I just gave the Earth away.

Journey's End

'Shouldn't be too long now Tom, It's been a bit of a drag hasn't it?'

'Sure has James, it's been a long journey, longest journey ever I should think.'

'Just think Tom if we hadn't had that visit, this trip wouldn't have been possible'

'True, we were so near. But we would never have got here without help. Who would have expected God to put in an appearance?'

'Well Tom, he did tell us before but nobody took any notice.'

'You're right James, even I knew that, and I was never involved.'

'I wonder what it will be like? I mean it is a step in the dark even for us. I wonder if they will be anything like us?'

'Even with all my knowledge and power I can't answer that one James, but you will find out soon enough.'

'Yes Tom, now we have solved this hyperspeed problem the universe is our oyster.'

'I am just thinking about what it used to be like before God came, Tom. Nobody believed in him, well hardly anyone. Even when he arrived there were still doubters.

They soon changed their minds though, didn't they? Especially when he demonstrated his power?

'They did indeed James. No option really, had they?'

'I can't help thinking about the mess we were in. All that self-inflicted disease which was out of control; the total breakdown of society; the loss of morality and family life; all the wars. My goodness, we were in a mess Tom. I reckon God knew we were near the end and that if he didn't step in we would be doomed. Funny wasn't it that the scientists and engineers, who always denied God, suddenly changed their minds when he started giving them the answers to their unsolved problems. They were so near to solving many problems, but would never have done it without help. The strangest thing was that when God explained who he was and where he came from, they had no problem understanding and accepting him. The answers to our questions had been there – but we were all too clever to see the answers before our eyes.'

'Yes James it really shook a lot of folks. Still, he has been very fair. The ones who caused all the problems couldn't expect to get away with it, could they? I think he has a superb method of justice and punishment.'

'Well you would Tom, you are totally in the clear. I wonder if they will be like us, I mean will they have two arms two legs, will they have fingers, toes, two ears, eyes nose and mouth just the same as we have? Well not like you Tom, but you know what I mean.'

'Yes I know what you mean James, we will be finding out what they are like soon enough now.'

'Okay Tom, I am switching you off now, I want you to concentrate on bringing the diplomats out of hibernation ready for when we land.

You can also double-check the navigational calculations, and do a quick run over your other functions. I will switch your verbal communication system back on in good time.'

'Right James, speak to you later.'

'Tom get a look at this, we are bang on course, you have done a great job.'

'Well James I only do what you tell me to.'

'Yes Tom but you do it so well. It looks beautiful doesn't it? They were right about the colour too, it's just like our own planet. A lovely blue.'

'Yes James it is truly beautiful, it gets nicer as it gets bigger.'

'I am finding this very emotional Tom, that is something you will never be able to understand'

'I am starting to understand James, I really am; It is a little difficult for me to speak at the moment.'

'Tom we will not try any communicating with the natives until we have safely landed, they will not have any idea of our arrival. I wonder if they have animals similar to ours? It's all very exiting now isn't it?

'It sure is James, I am getting excited too.'

'Tom I wonder if God ever visited here? I wonder why they decided to call this place "The Earth"?'

Tom didn't answer either question.

Too Long a Road

I run past Knockin-Kelly, with a pain in my belly
Well that's not true, I had pain everywhere.
Then on down the hill, I'd a promise to fill –
If I'd known then – I'd have spoken with care.
Down passed the church and onward I lurch
The pain more intense as I run, I am too old for this
My life should be bliss –
What a fool, just what have I done?
Then it's round Whiting Bay, wet through with the spray
My misery getting worse all the time,
When I think back those years as I do through my tears
I should be home with a nice glass of wine.
It was Five years ago when I uttered those words
The words that would cause me such dread,
'Will you come back when you're seventy
And run a 10k'? 'Cause I will – that's no problem' I said.
Little did I know what that time would bring
With the toll of each passing year,
I should have thought deeper before I opened my mouth
I just spoke with bravado I fear.
It was three weeks ago when my friend rang me up
'It's the race at the end of November'
What's he talking about I thought to myself?
Then I slowly began to remember.
So I push on round the bay, legs feeling like lead,
When the turning point comes into view.
Just over three miles, and then I can stop
I push on – what else can I do?
Old Doctor McGrath looks over his gate
Attired in sporran and kilt
He looks on with dismay as I run on my way
Cos my legs are beginning to wilt,
Then the church looms again and I know I'm on track
Not long to go now – what a thrill
Then comes great despair as I look ahead –
All I see is that bloody great hill.
Ten minutes later and over the brow.
Kings Cross is just one mile away

Staggering now round those last four bends;
I just hope I can run on the day?
It's not just the race that I promised to do,
There's something else I re-call that I did;
I made a large bet all those long years ago –
And I'll be damned if I'll lose that five quid.

*PS. I ran the Abbey Dash twenty years ago in a time of 37minutes.
In 2003, I ran it in 51 minutes, in 2006, in 55 minutes 10 seconds.*

This is definitely my last competitive run.

An Enigma

A bird in the hand gathers no moss

Eternity is not too long
And infinity is not very far
So you can keep your wondrous Gods
And I will keep my lovely car.
Don't talk to me of light speed
Of singularities and such –
And even big black holes
Don't bother me too much
We've just been taken for a ride
We're not really here at all
It's all a prelude to an overture
And we're just about to fall
You may not really comprehend this
Because life's not what it seems
I'm going now to find that bush
That will return me to my dreams.

The Old Age Problem Sorted

'Well what do you think then gentlemen? Shall we go over the main points again? Would you care to read out what we have down so far Mr Secretary.'

'Yes Mr Prime Minister. The six of you seem to broadly agree – these are the main points that have been raised. The over seventies can be regarded as a general burden and nuisance, contributing very little if anything to society or to the government. They are though very proficient at demanding their rights and taking from us. We find a considerable amount of the health budget is taken up with this group.'

'Okay let's discuss what we have so far. James?'

'The general opinion is that the elderly are just a bloody nuisance all round. Go out on the roads, there is always some silly old bugger in front of you with all the time in the world. They can't see properly, nearly all deaf as posts, and they dither about on roundabouts, a real menace. Go shopping and they are always there blocking the aisles with their bloody trolleys or Zimmer frames. They block the pavements with their shuffling about, and take all the seats. And they are always wanting more – never bloody satisfied.'

'Okay, got your point James, what's your take Tom'?

'Let's take a look at the fiscal side. A large slice of the health budget is taken up by the over-seventies with replacement parts. Just think what we could save there. How many knees, hips, legs and other things do they have fitted? They keep having bloody strokes and heart attacks, it shouldn't be like that; soon they will be living for bloody ever. What about eyes? Take all these cataract operations, they're bad enough but soon we could have eye replacement, what about that cost? Just think what we could do for AIDS, drug abuse and unmarried mothers if we had that money. What about care homes and nursing homes, how much do they cost to run? I know we have cut food and care to the bone, but all these bloody silly old fogies who don't know whether they are coming or going – I mean, what is the bloody point? They don't even know what day it is.'

'Yes, you're right on those points James, but we won't gain much from their pensions. They are so low now, it won't make much difference. How should it be done then? What do you think Tarquin?'

'The legislation should say that on reaching the age of seventy, life will be terminated. People will soon get used to the idea and any initial opposition will soon end. In fact in many cases it will be welcome. All property should be forfeit at death – that will be a nice little earner, and will help the overcrowding problem no end. Just think of how many dithering old fools are living in large properties, sometimes on their own – just doesn't make sense does it? But I have to ask about exception to the rule, we surely must have some exceptions, and will it be retrospective?'

'Okay Tarquin, thanks. Exceptions – Mildred, can you come in on that?'

'Well yes, we have thought of that. If anybody is considered essential to the state there could be a stay. We will also make it possible to buy time. The PM and myself discussed this earlier. We were thinking in the region of thirty thousand for a year. That should give the likes of us a good few years, but still get rid of the rest. There will be no state aid of any kind during this extension though, all health needs and care will be provided and paid for by the individual. With regards to applying it – a bit tricky that one, but we will have to feed it in gradually to keep them all happy. We will be fair of course.

Tarquin interrupted. 'What do they do in Wales and Scotland, Prime Minister have you had any feedback on this kind of thing?'

'No – and I don't bloody care to have either. They chose to go their own way and look what happened to the fools. They were in a right bloody mess last I heard. Sod 'em, that's what I say.'

'What about Europe, PM?' Ben asked.

'Don't know that either; since we made that final break, nobody seems to know what they do over there, and let's face it, who bloody cares anymore? I certainly don't. I remember when we nearly lost it because of those European fools. Let them sink now, and I hope it's without bloody trace.

'Well okay then guys, we seem to have a good starting point; we will put it to the executive committee. I think we are on to a winner here. Let's face it we haven't much alternative have we, with all the money the youngsters are demanding these days and hardly any of them willing to work. Yes, Ben?'

'I was thinking about all the kids the youngsters are producing. Something has to give. We are acting sensibly here, and let's face it we are in a better position to confront the old than the young. But just one point: what if the executives turn it down?'

'Stuff 'em, we say what goes on here, they are just a bunch of thick bloody noddies anyway, if they don't play ball I will sack the bloody lot of 'em. Yes Tarquin? But just a quickie.'

'What about any money or legacies that oldies want to leave?'

'I think to be fair, let's say ten percent of any assets will be allowed for buying time, anything over that to be forfeited. If time is bought, no other benefits can be passed on to family. Why should anyone be handed money for nothing – it's about time all that stopped, and then that will be another nice income for us. Who knows where this might lead if we get it up and running? There are a few other groups who spring to mind who we could well do without. We could have a real bloody shake up. Best do a bit at a time though.'

'Yes PM, we could end up being able to afford quite a few extra years I should think.'

'Right, let's break for lunch. I hear they have just got a new consignment of wine in from Australia that is very friendly to the old taste buds. Oh, you want to come back in Tom before we go?'

'I was just thinking about Australia, PM. That was a bloody good move when you emptied the prisons and sent all the wasters down there. It was similar to what happened years ago I understand.'

'Yes indeed, but it's been a financial success for us this time. Saved us a bloody fortune, and let's face it the Aussies soon turned it to their advantage – got the buggers working didn't they? And they keep asking for more of 'em, still – sooner a nice bottle of plonk than prisons full of useless criminals draining all our bloody resources.

'Okay, let's go and eat.'

Precious Memories

Yesterday was such a lovely day,
Walking miles along a country way.
Paddling together in the chilling streams;
Playing games that came right out of dreams.
Daisy chains, and watching butterflies,
Holding hands, and looking to the skies.
Young together, and yet without a care;
These memories that I so gladly share.
I don't suppose that you remember me –
Or days long gone when we were young and free.
Oh yesterday was such a lovely day,
How sad that it was not allowed to stay.

On a Wedding

You are starting a journey today
You could say it's a mystery tour,
No one can tell where you're going
Or know what life has in store.
I can tell you the road is a long one
And problems appear on the way,
So make sure you know all the road signs
And from the road try not to stray.
The first sign you will meet is the red one
This one you have to obey,
And usually after a reasonable time
It's quite safe to proceed on your way.
The most important sign is the amber
It glares out its warning to you,
There is no future in being a gambler!
You know only too well what to do.
The green sign means go, but beware of the road
Hazards can sometimes appear,
So keep well alert even on green
And round any problems you'll steer.
Don't be tempted to go down the road too fast
Let the wise guys go on their way.
You will enjoy the route more at a steadier pace
And the penalties you won't have to pay.
If the road starts to get very difficult
Pull into the side for a rest.
You really shouldn't get over heated,
To cool it right down is the best.
If you come across someone requiring help
To stop is the right thing to do.
Nobody gets a clear run on this road,
The next one for help could be you.
If you observe all these signs,
And take things in your stride
You shouldn't have too much to fear.
But whatever you do, please remember –
Make sure that you're always in gear.

A Young Boy's Memories of WW2

I remember when the streets were cobbled, so that the horses could get purchase to pull the coal carts, and the dustbin carts. I remember having to walk fifty yards up the street to get to the lavatory. We had no bathroom. Clothes had to be boiled in a coal-fired tub to get clean. We didn't have a fridge or vacuum cleaner and only hot water if the coal fire was lit. The only way we could cook was with a fire-side oven, or one gas ring. If it was a hot summer day – tough!

There were houses in my street that didn't have electricity, only gas. If they were lucky enough to have a radio it was powered by an accumulator, which was recharged each week. All streetlights were gas. My mother ironed the clothes with a flat iron this had to be placed in the fire to heat it – once again, if you didn't have a fire going, tough. In winter we used to take plates out of the oven wrapped in cloths and put them in the beds to keep warm. Only the one room with the fire was heated. Coal was difficult to get, so if you had no coal because you had run out, or had no money, tough. That meant no hot water, no cooking, no heating, no ironing and no bath.

All food was rationed – we were only allowed small amounts of lard, margarine, meat, bacon, and cheese, and only if they were available. Fruit was only for those who grew their own, i.e. apples, pears, plums. That meant that most people who lived in the cities never saw any fruit. Milk was not officially rationed but the deliveryman always made sure that most of his allowance went to new mothers and very young children. For the rest it was dried milk out of a can – a revolting concoction. Later in the war a small bottle of milk was given to schoolchildren. Sweets were available but were also rationed – our sweet coupons were always exchanged for things like tea and sugar. So although there were sweets in the shops, they were for the lucky few. Although England had television before the war, this was stopped when war broke out and people had to rely on wireless sets and cinema. The cinema was the entertainment for most people, but you had to be ready to evacuate if the air raid alarm went

Anywhere that was long enough for enemy planes or gliders to land was criss-crossed with ditches. That included all playing fields. We would try to jump across the ditches, but mostly we fell in. They were about six feet across, about ten feet long and about four feet deep. Most had muddy water in the bottom.

There were no signposts, no city or town signs, and of course no lighting of any kind after dark. All houses had blackout blinds and woe betide if any glimmer of light escaped. If there was no moon it was totally black outside.

Small torches and subdued lights for vehicles were allowed if there were no air raid alerts. Many roads, I remember, had large concrete blocks across them, or blocks ready to drag across in case of invasion. At night when the sirens sounded we were sometimes allowed a quick peep through the edge of the blinds. The flares that the Luftwaffe dropped were really bright and seem to hang in the sky for ages. Then it was into the cellars or shelters. We didn't like moonlit nights, although it was much better for seeing when outside, the Germans pilots used the moon to follow rivers to their destinations. We could hear the anti-aircraft guns firing in the small park about four hundred yards away.

Mrs Johnson lived near the bottom of our street, and on Saturday mornings I would do some errands for her. She used to give me a white sealed envelope and direct me to the shop over the tramlines at the bottom of the street. This shop was across three main roads; but there was never any traffic on them. I never dared look in the envelope. When I got to the shop I was instructed to make sure there was no one in before entering. 'Mrs Johnson sent this,' I said every week. The grumpy old shopkeeper took the envelope looked inside, grunted, then took something from under the shop counter, placed it in a bag, and told me never to let anyone see inside. I looked of course, and it was always a large bar of chocolate. The number of times I planned to run away to just get that bar of chocolate; but I never did. I always prayed though that Mrs Johnson would give me a piece, she never did!

When I delivered the bag intact to her house, she would then give me another bag which had cloths inside; and yes – another sealed envelope. This time I had to go to Mrs Godlove (I can see her now) a kindly fat Jewish lady, who had a greengrocers shop on the top crossing. I handed the envelope over again, after making sure of course that there was nobody in the shop. (Why there should be anybody in the shops I could not imagine, because there were never any goods on display in them!) Mrs Godlove opened the envelope as if it was a letter and always looked surprised. She then did the under the counter trick, and I was sent on my way, with the instructions to guard the contents of the bag with my life. I knew what was in the bag of course and always stopped round the corner to look in awe at the contents – six eggs. I had no idea how much was paid for this treasure, and it has always puzzled me why I was trusted with the packages, because I used to spend more time on the floor than on my feet! However I always got them back in one piece. I had never tasted an egg, or certainly couldn't remember if I had, but they looked wonderful.

Mrs Johnson took the bag from me as if it held the crown jewels, told me never to tell anybody, and gave me fourpence. We had eggs of course, well sometimes, but they came out of a tin. The texture was something like sawdust, my mother used to mix this concoction with water, then fry it and tell it us it was fried egg. It didn't matter though because the bread that we had to eat with it was definitely made from sawdust, and it took a saw to cut it.

The highlight of my week was Saturday afternoons at the 'Bughutch' (our local cinema) courtesy of Mrs Johnson's fourpence. This was when we all let off steam. I hope my memory doesn't desert me now, but I seem to remember seeing Flash Gordon, The Three Stooges, The Bowery Boys, The Dead-end Kids, Charlie Chaplin, Laurel and Hardy, The Marx Brothers. Was it Hop along Cassidy, and Gabby? Mickey Rooney and Judy Garland were very young, as were James Cagney and Edward G Robinson. If we had seen a cowboy film we used to fashion guns out of bits of old wood, if it had been a pirate film we would make swords. It's amazing what we could make out of bits of wood. Then we would knock hell out of one another. We were tough kids.

We laughed later at the antics of the likes of Jerry Lewis and Danny Kaye but never seemed to laugh with the same urgency that we did during the war.

School was about two miles away and we walked twice a day. Mostly there was no fuel for the boilers so we sat three to a two person desk and rotated every fifteen minutes to keep warm. They were hard times. We had ration books for everything, including clothing. It seemed that when we had coupons we had no money, and when we had money we had no coupons.

If the boats made it across, we sometimes had Canadian jam. This was in big tins and tasted awful, but we were grateful. I seem to remember living on jam and bread for years. We had some nice hot summers during the war, and sometimes the teachers would risk taking the children to the woods for a picnic. We would get a bottle of water and put a spoonful of Canadian jam in the bottle, then shake it vigorously and pretend it was lemonade. We would then eat our jam sandwiches and drink our coloured water under the trees.

I remember when there were bombs falling and anti-aircraft guns banging away, gathering shrapnel in the streets and swapping it at school. Shrapnel was both our toy and currency. During a heavy raid we could hear the shrapnel landing on the roofs and we knew we would be in for a treat the next morning. We would be out early to gather the jagged remains of shells and bombs, carefully grading and storing them. Later, towards the end of the war, we would swap army badges, bullets, bayonets, or anything to do with the war. I had a German army helmet with a swastika and eagle on it.

Sometimes school lessons were in air raid shelters. I remember being dragged to our reinforced cellar, when the air raid sirens started at night. It was not possible to sleep. The cellar was cold, damp, dark, and had no beds. We could be there for hours.

We would walk round the bombed areas in the daylight. One night it was our hospital, town hall, electricity station, and local pub that was bombed. I walked down to the city centre in the morning; incendiary bombs had been dropped during the raid and the town was still on fire. Part of the hospital had disappeared. The area where I lived had a tank factory, a munitions factory, an aircraft factory and heavy engineering works, plus a major railway junction, obviously a good target area – but I have to say we escaped quite lightly compared to some areas. All the kids could tell the enemy planes from our own by the different sounds of the engines, we could also identify aircraft by their silhouette. We were smart kids.

I can remember listening to the speeches of Adolph Hitler, Mussolini, and Lord Haw-Haw (William Joyce). He was an American-Englishman who transmitted propaganda radio messages to England from Germany, telling us we were doomed and that we must surrender. He was caught and hanged after the war for being a traitor.

The battle of Britain ended then in October 1940, (although we still suffered from less heavy air raids). We had fought alone and defeated the Luftwaffe – but only just, we were on our knees. The Spitfires and Hurricanes had performed superbly in the hands of our gallant pilots, and decimated the German bombers. If Hitler had known our true state he would have increased his effort, and the outcome could have been very different. The indiscriminate terror of the V1 and V2 rockets however were still some time away, and these awful weapons were yet to rain down on England.

So the Battle of Britain ended and we were now to start the Battle of the Atlantic. Hitler's navy would starve us to death if he couldn't do it with bombs. His U-boats nearly succeeded here as well; we relied on imports and were not getting any. Our Merchant Navy losses were more than we could sustain: 2,800 merchant ships were sunk. It was thanks to the increase in our naval power and the eventual destruction of the U-boat bases by land forces, that the Battle of the Atlantic was brought to an end. Once more we had survived – just …

The cars used coal gas or methane. The gas couldn't easily be compressed at that time, hence the large inflated bags on top of the cars. Petrol was only available to military vehicles, and emergency vehicles. These included police, ambulance, and fire engines. Our doctor even used a bicycle. If you had a car, and were desperate to drive, then you had to be rich enough to have a conversion to gas. Some cars had wood-burning steam engines. There were not many cars about.

Gas masks were horrendous things. They obviously had to fit very tight, and had a small window to see through, which always steamed up. They were extremely claustrophobic, and breathing was difficult because of all the filters in them. The worst part was having to go through the travelling gas chamber to test them. These large vehicles came round periodically, and everybody hated them. We had to put our masks on and walk through a gas filled chamber, nobody knew what would happen if they leaked, and nobody bothered to tell us. Fortunately gas was never dropped, but we wore our gas masks quite a lot, and had to carry them everywhere until the end of the war. Some people refused to carry them, but risked being fined if caught without them.

Small boys love fishing and we were not going to be deprived of it by a war. Large water tanks that resembled swimming pools were everywhere. During air raids water mains were often fractured and these water tanks were the emergency supplies. They were netted over to stop small boys diving in. Being bright boys we fashioned pieces of wood, string, and bent pins and went fishing. We spent hours sat on the sides of these tanks with our strings in the water, waiting for that big catch, which we had been told had been spotted many times. We spoke about Spitfires, Mosquitoes and Hurricanes, but we didn't know we needed worms on our bent pins –

Coded messages on the radio were a real challenge. They went out on normal programmes. We boys were brilliant at decoding them:

The cows will be sleeping gently tonight
Uncle Tom has broken his leg, but will still play

These are not verbatim, but that's what they were like. We listened and quickly worked out the codes. I don't know how we did it because the Germans never broke the codes, only the ones they were meant to. We were part of the war all right.

Spies of course were everywhere, and we boys were experts at spotting them. Anybody who was not instantly recognised was of course a spy. We trailed them for miles. We spotted swastikas on cigarette packets, and Lugers hidden in pockets. We didn't miss much. We didn't see any Americans until a long time after the Pearl Harbour attack by the Japanese in December 1941. We had strict instructions to keep away from them. Our parents said we looked like urchins. Well we may have done; but we didn't know what urchins looked like, so we took no notice, and after school if there were no raids on, we would hightail it to Chapelgate.

This area was about two miles away, but we soon covered the ground. With our arms out to the sides, and making the appropriate noises we became Spitfires and Hurricanes, complete with machine gun and cannon noises. Many a dogfight took place between our house and Chapelgate. Chapelgate was the posh area; we couldn't understand why the 'Yanks' got the posh area to live in.

When we arrived at Chapelgate, we would work out our strategy and select our methods of operation. These were only single missions and had to be executed with great skill. When a Yank was spotted (always recognised by his smart uniform) the elected urchin would saunter casually up, and in his best American would utter the magic words 'Got any gum chum?' I have to say we were fairly successful and very rarely returned from mission empty mouthed. It's a good job because this was the nearest we would get to sweets for a long time.

My wife used to go with her mother to work in the fields near a German prison camp, and although she was told not to go anywhere near the prisoners, being a normal little girl she would take no notice and would often go to talk to them. She told me that they were always kind and made a fuss of her. Some could speak a little English.

I suppose most of those Germans eventually returned safely to their own country and families. But I often wonder how many of the Yanks who were destined to cross the channel on D-Day and who used to give us urchins chewing gum in Chapelgate never made it back home?

It may all sound pretty horrendous, but remember I never knew anything different. It was after the war ended before I first went in a motor car. I cannot remember ever going out of our city. I can only remember going in tramcars. For most people it was a long time after the war ended before things got any easier, and it was a very slow process.

When I see what children have today; where they travel to, and how they dress, and they still never seem to be satisfied – I must admit my mind sometimes goes back to those days.

Post Script.

On the 7th May 1945, although the announcement hadn't officially been made we knew the war in Europe was over. All the children went to school in their best clothes. I remember mine had patches on them – so had many other children's clothes. My shoes were badly split at the back, as my feet were growing they pushed the heels out. I don't know if it was lack of money or lack of clothing coupons but it was a long time before I had shoes that fitted me properly. My socks were always darned too. Many children didn't have any shoes at all, I can remember seeing them walking about in bare feet. A special fund was set up to supply 'Boots for the Bairns'. I suppose then that I was one of the lucky ones.

We were sent home from school and so had two days off – May 8th was declared an official national holiday. We were on double summer time during the war and it didn't get dark until about ten in the evening. After all the street parties were over, it seemed that every house had their black out curtains removed and all had their lights on – this was quite an amazing sight for me and many others who could not remember ever seeing the streets lit up at night. That day seemed to last forever. On that day I also heard church bells ring for the first time.

Victory in Europe was ours then – but victory in the Pacific was still to be won. I still had relatives out there in the forces and so had many other families. I didn't know at the time of course but my future wife did not see her father for six years, from being two years old to being eight. She also had an uncle who was a POW in Burma. Many families found it very difficult to celebrate until they knew their loved ones were safe, and many of course could never celebrate.

It was wonderful to go to bed that night and know that there would be no more guns banging – no more bombs dropping, and to know I could look forward to seeing my first banana. Little did I know just how long that would take – or how long it would be before I could even go and buy sweets again. The war had taken a terrible toll on our country.

War is indeed a nasty business.

Ariadne

Pride, Lust, Betrayal, Bestiality and Magic – it's all here.

King Minos had young Daedalus
Build him a labyrinth of clay.
There he placed the Minotaur –
With young boys and girls to prey.
Pasiphae was married to Minos
And the Minotaur was her son –
But not the son of Minos
The King had been outdone.
Minos refused to honour Poseidon
Poseidon was not too chuff
So he looked to get his own back
And searched for a bit of rough.
Pasiphae was feeling fruity
And found Minos, oh so dull.
So she took herself off searching!
And found herself a bull.
So the Minotaur's mum was Pasiphae
And the Bull he was the dad –
Then on the scene came Theseus,
A proud young Athenian Lad.
Theseus went to save his friends,
And slay this horrid thing –
Ariadne fell in love with him,
And produced a sword and string.
So the Minotaur did come to grief,
At the hand of Theseus fair
Then Theseus followed the magic thread
And found Ariadne waiting there.
Ariadne and Theseus did run away
To an island surrounded by blue –
It seemed they were made for each other,
Their love just seemed so true.
But Theseus was so young and strong,
His wings he had to spread.
So he upped and left Ariadne
On Naxos, asleep in her bed.

But Ariadne wasn't over-grieved
She liked a wine or two,
So when Dionysus came on the scene
She said 'Oh my God – you'll do.'

Dionysus, the son of Zeus, married Ariadne on Naxos.

The Damsel

A triplet

Methought the damsel fair of face
Hair in ribbons, dressed in lace
Shaped in a way my hand could trace.
Perchance that she would'st look my way
Her wondrous beauty, my eyes do pray –
'Twer possible she'd note my sway.
Methinks her loveliness so strong
How can'st my feelings then be wrong?
Her heavenly grace do'st urge me on.
Could'st she, my dream, belong to me?
My vice-gripped heart would'st then be free;
To give my love, my soul, for thee.

The Prison

Nico and Ianis were silent, but both were deep in thought. Nico knew his thoughts would not be the thoughts of his prison companion. He had not yet, even after nine months got to the stage where he could call Ianis his friend. He remembered in great detail the speech they were given by the governor on the morning they had arrived.

'*Listen carefully and remember well. You are all repeat criminals. You are here because it was decided this was the best place for you. This is an evil place–you will hate it. I hate it, my men hate it, we have to be here because of you lot – so we hate you. The only consolation we have is that we can go home to our wives and families, and have a cold beer when we feel like it. You lot are here for at least two years, there will be no cold beer for you.*

'*You will be well fed here, not tasty food, but adequate to keep you healthy and strong – you will need to be strong. First thing then; there is no escape from here. The two-mile track you have just been brought up is always guarded and lit up at night. My men are armed and are ordered to shoot on sight – there is no escape that way. You have probably looked out to sea and wondered. Let me put you right on that score. There is nothing here that will help. You will sleep on iron framed beds, there is no wood here – nothing that will float. It is not possible to swim more than two hundred yards out from the shore before the current will have you; there is no escape there.*

You will also have looked at the cliffs. Four hundred feet high and not climbable – believe me, the climb has been attempted many times by fully equipped and trained climbers – no one has got near to the top. You will not escape from here, so don't bother to even think about it. Harbour no thought of 'Devils Island' and 'Alcatraz'. You will only leave here when your sentence is over, or you die first.

'*You will not be locked up. The cells hold two prisoners, you will have your clothes, one thin mattress and nothing more. There are no walls to the cells only a roof. The perimeter fence is electrified – just don't go near it. You will work in the quarry under armed guards at all times. You will have picks and sledge hammers. One day half of the prisoners will break rocks, the next day they will cement them back together. You will do this every day for the duration of your sentences. Do not be tempted to injure yourselves. The hospital building which you will have noticed with its red crosses is just a cell with walls. We have no doctor, just a medical orderly who is useless – no drugs of any kind. Just stay clear of injuries. The mosquitoes you will get used to.*

'*You will have noticed the cages. These are used for infringements – they are not nice places to visit. Anyone unfortunate to be sent to a cage will be very sorry. The cages have nooses hung from the top spars. We have various ways of using them depending on the severity of the infringement. The methods: hanging by the chin, toes just on the ground. Hanging by the arms toes just on the ground. The worst punishment is hanging by one leg and one arm completely suspended. You will be naked and have no food or water. The cages are completely open to the elements, blistering sun or cold wind and rain – there is no avoiding the elements. One day is usually the most anyway can take. Just don't go there. Finally don't make any friends; you will never know who you can trust. We have rewards for information – any good steer can earn a prisoner two iced cans of beer – most will sell their mothers or children for just one can of beer. I have been honest with you. We are not totally cruel. Behave, do your work, no escape attempts, and it is possible to survive.'*

Nico had gone over that welcome speech a hundred times, looking for something that he might have missed or a clue of some kind. Six months had blown his mind – he had to get out. He decided he had to have friends. He would have to take the risk. Ianis was his first risk. He seemed okay – they had got on well together and supported each other through their dark times, of which there had been many. Nico broached the subject of escape to Ianis just lightly at first and he was astounded by the response. Ianis had also been thinking the same way himself but had been too scared to tell Nico. Slowly a plan was worked out. Ianis was a good swimmer and was all for swimming out. Nico who used to do a lot of climbing had been studying the cliff at every chance and was convinced that was the way out.

Over the weeks Nico coached Ianis in climbing techniques. He was a quick learner and Nico knew if he could make it, Ianis would make it also, following on closely behind. There was a part of the cliff hidden from the camp, and body counts were seldom made after the return from work; they would have enough time before it got too dark – but it would be a close thing and very risky.

When Nico had taught Ianis all he could about free climbing he knew that the time had come to enlist another friend. They had to clear the electric fence and needed help to do this. They chose the guy who they thought was the best risk and most likely able to help them. To their delight he agreed, but insisted no one else should be aware of the escape attempt. He would not be going with them, but would stay behind and cover the escape attempt.

Alexis was as good as his word; the prisoners were in their cells mostly sleeping off the day's hard labour. The guards were drinking their cold beer. The road was floodlit – and the guards on duty there were well-armed. The fence nearest to the cliff was never checked, after all there was no escape there. Nico and Ianis eased their way under the now safe fence. As soon as they were clear Alexis reconnected the electricity supply and tidied the escape point. With no tracks, no one would ever know.

The climb started almost immediately, fairly easy at first but getting progressively harder. About half way up Nico was delighted at the progress. Ianis was strong and was following every toe and hand hold that Nico used. About one hundred feet from the top Ianis was in trouble as the hand and footholds were now much smaller and giving him great problems.

Nico was having problems too and he marvelled at how Ianis had done. He offered his friend all the support he could but it could only be verbal, there was no way he could physically help him. Ianis lasted only another couple of feet and then fell backwards. Nico watched as his friend bounced off the lower cliff and plunged into the sea. With only himself, to worry about Nico concentrated on not making any mistakes, He could fully understand why this cliff had not been climbed before. He knew that although he was an expert climber this cliff was one he would have never tried to do – it was just far too difficult and risky. He was only doing it now out of necessity – a different ball game.

Nico knew he had made it with about twenty feet to go. He had scanned the top section and realised it would be possible. He would not be missed until morning roll call; all being well he would be miles away and well out of it. He had it all planned – his escape from the island in a small fishing boat, there would be plenty of those around the coast. He could island hop all the way up to the mainland and then he would never be traced. He might even leave Greece altogether. He was feeling life was about to change: just the last few feet over the top and then a well-earned rest.

Nico never heard the bang; the bullet hit him in the forehead. He described the same arc as Ianis had – hitting the same outcrop and splashing into the sea at the same spot.

Alexis was excused labour the next day – he would find his two tins of ice cold beer much more to his liking than breaking those bloody rocks.

The Long Trek

The road ahead seemed endless,
As he pulled the straps tight on his pack.
The dog snuggled down on his shoulder,
And he knew there was no going back.
It seems ages since the accident,
When they shot through the door with a slam,
With his mum screaming loud through the window,
As down the front path they both ran.
He knew that his dog would be hungry,
And would soon expect to be fed.
They could eat what he had in his pocket,
But what would they do for a bed?
He had a long talk to the dog in his arms,
They decided they had better go home.
Maybe it would start to get dark soon,
And they shouldn't be out on their own.
As they cautiously made their way back up the path,
His mother appeared at the door.
'Before either of you can have any tea,
You can clear all this mess from the floor –
That pup is tearing my house apart,
Don't teach him any more tricks.
And don't go to the end of the street again,
Remember you're only just six'.

The Human Race.

Up and running, gaining speed
Sole intention is to lead.
White ones black ones brown ones too
With other colours showing through.
Must charge on, no mercy given
To get in front, they are all driven.
Anything goes in this mad race
Strive for position, maintain the pace.
Gun and bullet sword and spear
Anything to cause great fear.
Death no problem, a trivial thing
Only thought the race to win.
Children and elderly don't count at all
Collateral damage – they have to fall.
Arms and legs off – what a shame
But if it helps achieve our aim!
Buildings fall, planes blown apart
It doesn't pay to have a heart.
Women just don't mean a thing,
Well a moment's pleasure they sometimes bring.
Kids can be used to clear the way,
If they're blown up, it makes their day.
Napalm weapons – precision bomb
How can these things be ever wrong?
We must make sure the race we win
And never be accused of sin.
Surging on, such a frightening scene
No thoughts at all of what might have been.
Objectives achieved in different ways
And even the weakest have had few delays.
Down on their knees now with prayers, thanks and grace,
As the fools near the end of the human race.

Envoi.
It's not the winning it's the part you play
No gain, if you lose your soul on the way.

The Hymn of the Deaf Mutes

From early last century.

Every Sunday morning two hundred silent voices sing a hymn of infinite pathos in St Bede's Church, Clapham Road London. It is called 'The Hymn of the Deaf Mute'. The men and women who sing it belong to London's army of silent people. Here is the first verse:

> *Unto our Father's house we come,*
> *Thy children we, though deaf and dumb.*
> *Although our ears no sound enjoy,*
> *Although our lips no speech employ;*
> *We kneel before Thy throne of grace*
> *And clasp thy feet in love's embrace.*

The Church has a great shell from the Philippines for a font, a gift to the four thousand deaf mutes of London.

A Rector of a Welsh Parish found a dead donkey on his land. He communicated the fact to the proper authorities and asked that the said donkey be removed. He received a reply saying that it was part of his office to bury the dead, and that they would look to him to do so.

    He sent the following reply: 'I will certainly do so, but I thought it my duty to inform the deceased's relatives first.'

In Newtown Linford Churchyard Leicestershire, there is a tombstone with nothing inscribed on it but the alphabet written in different styles. The stonemason submitted the lettering to a customer to select a style; the customer was so pleased with the appearance that he decided to have the original tombstone with nothing else added.

The vicar of the Parish of Orton-on-the-Hill in Leicestershire was hanged, drawn and quartered at Tyburn as recently as 1715. His name was William Paul. He attended Rugby College and then went on St John's College Cambridge. He was presented with the Parish of Orton by the Bishop of Oxford. His mistake was in joining the Jacobites. He was apprehended soon after joining and was taken to London for trial. He is thought to be the last clergyman to take his departure under this particular form of triple torture.

Alone amid the ruins stands a little English Church which is the only building left standing in the old Leper Colony of 'Robben Island' seven miles to the south of Cape Town South Africa. The poor unfortunate creatures 'the lepers' were removed to an asylum at Pretoria on the mainland where their keep was so much cheaper. After the evacuation every building in the compound was blown up, except the little church, which was the only building not owned by the government. This church still survives.

A Tombstone erected to the memory of a ragman in the church-yard of Wymondham near Oakhampton reads:
I in my time did gather rags
And many a time I filled my bags,
Although it was a ragged trade
My rags are sold and debts are paid.
Therefore go on don't waste your time
On bad biography and bitter rhyme –
For what I am this cumbrous clay assures
And what I was is no affair of yours

Situated in Grasmere in the heart of the English lakes is the beautiful church of St Oswald. Eight of the yew trees in the churchyard were planted by Wordsworth himself, and under the shadow of one of them is his grave, with the simple inscription, 'William Wordsworth, 1850. Mary Wordsworth 1859.' The next grave is that of their daughter Dora. The next but one is that of the poet's sister Dorothy. There are three doors to the church, the Clergy door, the west door for the men, and the south door for the women These doors are from the time when the men and women sat at different sides of the church. In the past it was the custom of the church to bury the dead in the church near their family pew.

The parish church of All Saints Cawthorpe, Yorkshire, contains a unique organ. One of the manuals of the organ has been fitted with black 'natural' keys and white 'sharp' keys'. Nobody seems to know why.
    The church itself is noteworthy because of the fragments of Anglo-Saxon crosses which have been built into its walls.

The parish of Colerne, Wilts has a black church cat called 'Timothy the second'. On Thursdays he always attends for choir practice. Every Sunday five minutes before the eleven o'clock service is due to commence, he goes to meet the Rector then jumps up and unlatches the vestry gate. He then escorts the Rector into the church. When funerals are in progress he always watches, but from a respectable distance. This church apparently does not have the proverbial 'church mouse'.

The lesson to be read should always be conned over beforehand, (by the way it is interesting to note that the Oxford English Dictionary defines the word 'con' as indicating to the steersman the course he should steer. That is good. The reader should always have an idea of the aim, purpose, and object of the lesson he is to read). So I say to you my brethren, with respect to your friends and family, always con them as much as possible.

Canon Trystram related this delightful incident which occurred in a church on the borders of Northumberland. The congregation was composed of mainly Cheviot shepherds accompanied by their dogs.

On this morning visitors from other churches, along with their dogs, had been invited to the service. When the sermon was finished some of the dogs got up and walked out of the church. When the blessing was finished more dogs rose and walked out. The remaining dogs walked out after the last hymn. Each dog had apparently followed the custom of his own church.

These vignettes were culled from a church magazine. This magazine, along with other old papers, was found in a corner of our loft in an old case. I hope you enjoyed reading these, and please keep in mind the date of origin when reading these little gems from the past.

PS. I actually saw this one myself whilst driving around the Mull of Kintyre in Scotland. Looking in a small graveyard I found a stone which just gave the name of the deceased, then underneath was inscribed '23rd Psalm', nothing else. What do they say about the Scots?

Stress and Beauty

I ran the moors this week, the weather warm and still.
Down the track, then through the gate, and on to the first hill.
Tiny rabbit now in front, does it want a race?
Then like a little miracle it disappears in space.
The sheep are looking worried; their lambs all bleating now.
The little calves are gorgeous but protected by mum cow.
The meadow is all natural, wild flowers of all hue –
A journey back to childhood – buttercups and bells of blue.
Through the gate and up the lane, start to feel it now
Legs start to object a bit – but push on to the brow.
Fifteen minutes not too bad – nearly at the top.
Legs are calling louder now, but no way will I stop.
First brow now behind me, a gentle slope downhill,
Take the cattle grid in full flow; start to feel the thrill.
The hawk is hovering overhead, eyeing me below –
It turns and dives; pure magic, what a super show.
The pheasant are all out in force as I battle on.
Curlews, Larks and Thrushes joining in the song.
Running by the stream now, see the bridge ahead.
Down the bank, over stump, then long jump over bed.
Heart sinks now, I spy the hill – looming to the sky
Loose shale now no grip at all – still I have to try.
Fox glares at me as if I'm mad, nothing else to say
Then as I draw up level it turns and skulks away.
Oh, pure joy – now at the top, what a super view
It really is God's country; I'd love to share with you.
Now down the lead mine spoil, what story it could tell.
Over the ford, last short rise, yes still doing well.
Check my watch – time okay, not too bad at all
This downhill part is stony, be careful not to fall.
Sweating now and breathing deep, breeze caressing face
Hope I will be fit enough – when I do the race.
Moorland is so beautiful, heather peeping through
In another fortnight, this area will be new.
Through the gates, losing time, but keep the cattle in
They'd really like to run with me, making an awful din.
End in sight now, stretching hard, half a mile to go
Starting to hurt all over – come on now do not slow.
Holding on, glance down at watch, last bit through the wood.
Home at last – fifty minutes. Wow that's pretty good.
PS. This was one my moorland training areas.

Gentler Days

I long for gentler days –
Those long lost gentler ways.
When children were a joy;
When we knew a girl from boy.
When words were so discreet –
No obscenity on the street,
When young girls were so sweet.

I long for the gentler time –
When I took a hand in mine;
The thrill of that first kiss
That heavenly feel of bliss;
The night I couldn't sleep
For those days now I weep –
Not for me – but those I keep!

I long for gentler things –
That innocence still brings
The kindness of a friend;
A love that will not end.
When we let things take their time;
Not – one night, and then be mine
This need for instant pleasure
Will rob you of life's treasure….

I long for gentler days –
I truly miss the ways,
The softer words and touch
Are things I miss so much.
The melody and tune,
And sweet words that made us swoon;
You can keep this mindless din
And the world that's steeped in sin.

I long for gentler pace
Had enough of life's rat race,
This striving for the best –
And to hell with all the rest;
Should this really be our quest?

I long for gentler days.
I pray for gentler ways ….

Dear Basil – Love Scamp

Poor Scamp had an unusual Problem. Some years ago a letter appeared in our church magazine. The letter was written by Basil, a rather nondescript old black mongrel dog. Basil had been rescued and was loved by, the Roman Catholic priest in the village. The magazine was a joint one shared between the entire Dale. Scamp must have read Basil's letter – and decided to reply. This is what appeared in the magazine.

Dear Basil,

My name is Scamp. I always read the church magazine each month. I obviously pricked up my ears when I read your letters. They don't seem to have many doggy letters. You obviously read the magazine too, so you may remember a poem about a doggy called Sadie, well Sadie is my sister, and I thought you might like to know a little about me.

Just before Christmas, I was taken into the doggy hotel at Adel. I had been badly treated. I don't remember a lot, only that I was very poorly and I hurt all over. The nice lady there took me straight to the doggy hospital and the doctor said he didn't think he could help me. Anyway he decided to try and I had a long operation. I then had to go back to the doggy hotel where they didn't expect me to live for long.

When I got back there they didn't have any room for me because it was Christmas and all the rooms were full. They put some straw into a drawer and laid me on it. I was so poorly I just didn't care. I remember some people coming with gifts for the doggies for Christmas, and the lady asked them if they would take me home. She explained that I was very poorly and needed special care. I overheard her say that it would be my last Christmas. I was eleven. Well they took me home for Christmas and I met Sadie. They were all nice to me and looked after me. After a long time I started to get a bit better. The people who took me home adopted me and became my mum and dad. I wouldn't let anyone touch me at first because I hurt so much and I was frightened, but now I let them touch me and tickle my belly, and sometimes I jump on the bed for a cuddle. My mum and dad have a holiday home in your village and I love going there. I can't chase rabbits like you Basil because my legs are too small and I have arthritis. But I love walking by the river and in the fields. I hope the editor of the magazine will publish this letter so you can read it, and maybe if you write back he will print your reply.

I want you to know that I am a lot better now. I still have problems that my mum and dad have to help me with and I also still have to take medicine for my tummy, but I am now a happy little doggy. I honestly believe I am in heaven! Well, when I am caught on the bed with my head on the pillows my mum, says, 'Our Scamp thinks he is in heaven.'

With lots of licks and wags,

Love, Scamp.

Yes it was true, Scamp had either been abused or medically neglected, we never found out which, but he was a very sick little dog. The operation that had saved Scamps life had left him with serious problems and these were explained to us before we took him home. We really didn't know if he would survive or not.

Scamp's injuries had been to his back end. He could wee okay but the operation to save him had meant he had lost the ability to use his rear department. It took a while to sort this problem out and I will not go into those details. Scamp did start to recover as you know and we had devised our method of helping him. First I must tell you he would only let my wife and I and our two daughters anywhere near him at this time. That meant that whatever the situation one of us had to be available. Journeys away had to be carefully planned to make sure one of us was always at hand for Scamp.

Scamp was able to convey his feelings to us. He had a certain way of looking and we instantly knew what he wanted. The poor little guy did have feelings and he was embarrassed and unhappy at his loss of dignity. His favourite walk was up in the woods and when he was ready he gave us the look – ears down, and an expression that clearly meant 'I am sorry but I can't do this on my own' He always went out of the way so no one would see him. The four of us knew exactly where to squeeze Scamp, and how hard to do it. When it was over Scamp's ears would go up – his tail would be wagging and he would shoot off for a run round the woods. This procedure was performed two or three times every day.

My wife was a little bit embarrassed about his problem at first, but all the other dog walkers in the woods soon got to know about Scamp and his problem, and they were very discreet. In fact Scamp soon became a firm favourite in the village. He used to wear a little kerchief around his neck and he looked a very dapper little guy whilst walking out.

Scamp was the most laid-back little terrier dog and would make friends with any dog and any person. 'Cassy' was the village bully. She was mean – with a capital M. No dog could approach her. Very few people either. She was a very large German Shepherd guard dog and knew it. One day Scamp went calling and somehow he got into Cassy's compound and invited himself into the house. He was found by Cassy's owner curled up asleep with her. He was none too pleased – if this got out she would lose her street cred. All the time we knew Cassy, Scamp was the only dog she would tolerate. Shirley and I made friends because of Scamp. We were part of a very select group. Cassy sadly had to be put to sleep after she badly mauled a very large Rottweiler. She was just too mean.

Scamp was lovely in the house and would make friends with anybody. But he could only be patted round his front end. He had lots of little tricks and frequently had us in stitches. People have often told us that they wouldn't have taken Scamp on with his problems. Well it was never seen as a problem to us, we just saw it as something that had to be done (not very pleasant for Scamp or us, but necessary). The pleasure and love that Scamp gave us was more than payment for what help we gave him.

Scamp lived to be nearly seventeen. Sadie died soon after.
RIP Scampy Doodle, and Sadie, And of course Cassy –

Morning Vignette.

Early morning
Walk in wood
Mist just clearing
Sun just rising
Birds all singing
Dog is running
All is well;
Not surprising!

Ode to an L-Driver

Don't rub the tyres on the kerb
That's really very naughty.
And when you arrive at a major road
Don't stop the car too shorty.
Don't let the car run back too much
The car behind won't like it.
And if you don't brake fast enough
You possibly could strike it.
Try and relax a little bit
Don't grip the wheel so tight
And don't drive through a red light again
It gave me such a fright.
I was impressed when you drove through town
At ninety miles an hour,
But next time dear – cool it a bit,
And drive at thirty, flower.
You're not really doing too bad to say
So don't get cross and jumpy.
It's not your fault – it's the clutch that's wrong
When the car goes shake and bumpy.
I promise to stick that gear stick
So it stays where it ought to be
I realise it's not fair on you
When it jumps up on my knee.
Now seriously my dear you are doing quite well
It's just not easy for ladies to drive.
But I am certain you will pass your test
If we manage to survive –

Everyone

Everyone wants to be your friend
But will stab you in the back.
Everyone needs to go straight on
They've forgotten how to tack.
Everyone needs to slow down
But still speeds everywhere.
Everyone needs to see everything
But never stops to stare.
Everyone works a computer today
But still doesn't know the score.
Everyone wants peace
But still has to be at war.
Everyone is a girl today
But wants to be a boy.
Everyone wants to be happy
But there's nothing to enjoy.
Everyone is an atheist
God does not have a part.
Everyone is caring
But no one has a heart.
Think deeply about these words
You will realise they are true,
But everyone of course –
Is not meant to include you ….

Rescue in the Dolomites

There are times in life when one has to take responsibility for a situation and make decisions accordingly – hoping they are the right ones. This was one such situation. All you will read is true, just has it happened.

My son Andrew had never skied before. He was to be married later in the year and I suggested we should have a last holiday together and go skiing. He thought this an excellent idea, seeing that I would be paying. My wife thought it was a good idea but the problem would be his future wife. She was not keen on him being out of her sight but she eventually relented when I explained that the object of the exercise was a last holiday together for father and son and an opportunity for Andrew to sample the delights of skiing.

I booked a holiday at Campitello di Fassa in the Italian Dolomites. The hotel was quite comfortable and after breakfast on the first day we went to be fitted out with our skiing gear. An hour or so later found us on the slopes and I was giving Andrew his first skiing lesson. I was what could be described as a medium ability, red slope skier. I taught Andrew the basics, and in a couple of hours he was skiing as well as I could. The week zoomed past and we sampled most of the runs in the area and had some great skiing.

On the last day we ventured further afield to an area we hadn't skied before. The cable car followed a black run for about a mile before we alighted. We were able to observe this run all the way up, it looked mean. We had a good day sampling the upper slopes, and made our way back to catch the last cable car descent of the day. The start of the black run was adjacent to the cable car, and I couldn't believe my eyes when Andrew turned right and headed on to the run. I wasn't about to see him on the black run on his own – so reluctantly I also headed that way. He stopped and waited at the point of no return, and I asked him what the hell he was doing. He just wanted to prove to himself that he could do it. There was no point in falling out because we had at least a mile of difficult skiing ahead. I told him if we took it very steady we should make it okay.

We had gone about four hundred yards and had stopped to view the next section, when we heard the screaming. Looking round we saw a skier bouncing down the centre of the piste. It was very steep and very icy. Each bounce was higher than the one before and he was heading for the right hand side of the run which had a sheer drop, protected by a safety net of about ten-foot. The way this guy was bouncing he would clear it with ease. We looked at one another and both said together, 'he is a dead'. The last bounce was actually kind to him and he hit the net just short of the top then crumpled to the ground. We skied down as fast as we could and were relieved to find him relatively unscathed.

We did know this guy by sight, he was actually staying in the same hotel. He had been with a party of friends but they had got separated. Intending to catch the last cable car, he had spotted Andrew and I set off down the black run and foolishly decided to follow. Unfortunately he had come to grief on the first difficult part and completely lost control, losing his skies in the process. A German skier had also seen the action and had collected the wayward skis and brought them to us. The young man groaning on the ground was called Dave, and he was just getting to his feet when the German arrived with his skis. On being asked, Dave said he was okay, we thanked the guy and he continued down. I told Dave the only course of action open to us was to carry on down the run to the bottom, I told him to put his skis back on and that we would make our way down slowly together. He then hit us with his reply; he was not putting his skis back on. He had bottled out, and also gone into shock – he was shaking quite badly.

While all this had been going on the last cable car down had gone past and no more skiers were about. I realised we could be in some trouble, and taking responsibility for the situation decided the best option at this time was to stick together. It was impossible to walk down the piste as it was too steep and icy. The only option was the left side, where the trees were – maybe there would be more purchase there and we could walk down between the trees. We very carefully traversed the piste and entered the wooded area carrying our skis. This was a tragic mistake; the area beneath the trees was icier than the piste and after a few yards we realised we were in serious trouble, our ski boots gave no purchase on the icy ground whatsoever. Dave quickly lost his skis and poles (or discarded them). Andrew and I were very careful to hang on to ours. We were now in a position where any movement – up down or sideways, was impossible; we were stuck and in real trouble.

It was now bitterly cold and I was extremely worried. Amazingly we were given a last chance of help; I heard a skier on the piste about twenty yards away and called out as loud as I could; what a relief it was when I heard him brake and stop. He was another German, who had missed the last cable car, and I think also the last guy on the piste, truly our last hope for help. He didn't speak English, so I had to explain in my poor German our predicament. He made the right responses and told me he would get help. We now had a waiting game, and it was rapidly getting dark. A competent skier would get down the slope from our position in five minutes. If the alarm had been raised we could hopefully be getting help within half an hour or so.

The police rescue squad were the first on the scene, and their arrival brought tremendous relief. These guys had actually come down from the top. (We never found out how they got there). They were not too kind, and were a bit arrogant – probably they thought with good reason. At this stage we wanted to be rescued not to have to explain the situation. The guy in charge got the message okay. He told us to walk out of the trees to the piste. I explained we couldn't move.

After a discussion in Italian with his colleagues, he shouted that he would send two officers in to lead us out. 'Don't send anyone in without ropes,' I shouted back. He just scoffed at this remark and the two officers approached us in the trees. They had gone about five yards when they both slipped on the ice and shot down between the trees on their backs. They were not injured, but they could not now move. There were now five men to rescue. The situation had turned very serious again.

A short time later we then heard the sound of motors – the Italian Mountain rescue team had arrived from below. I imagine the police squad were as pleased to hear that sound as we were. Fortunately the guy in charge of the police rescue squad and the guy in charge of the mountain rescue team both spoke good English. I called out to the new arrivals not to attempt a rescue without ropes. Fortunately they were well equipped. Using our skis and poles, we managed to help the mountain rescue team to our position in the trees, leaving ropes rigged behind them. Their first priority was to get the policemen out, as they were in the worst position. With ropes rigged up the rescue went fairly smoothly, and about half an hour later we now found ourselves on the black piste once more.

I asked the rescuers to get us down, and told them that I would explain the situation at the bottom, they agreed without question. Dave was shaking very badly now and he was quickly wrapped up and placed in a rescue sled. Andrew and I still had our skiing gear and we were asked if we could ski down to the bottom, it was about three-quarters of a mile. Andrew agreed to ski with assistance. I declined and opted for a rescue sled. There was very little light now and I just didn't feel competent to ski down. We all set off together. The mountain rescue team now took charge of the situation, with two men to a sled and the others close by. The police squad took position around the outside of the party. We stayed together all the way down, and I can tell you it was a hair-raising experience – very steep, very icy, and very frightening.

I cannot describe to you my feelings when we arrived at the bottom safely. The questioning then started, and I was at last able to explain to the rescuers that Andrew and I were only in that predicament because we had stopped to help Dave, who had taken a bad fall and had refused to put his skis back on. When they realised that Dave wasn't with Andrew and I and that we had only stopped to try to help him, their attitude changed completely. Dave was in no condition to be remonstrated with and the rescuers suggested he should maybe go to hospital for a check up. He was having none of this; he was due to fly home to Manchester the next day.

I gave a full account of the occurrence which was all taken down in writing, along with our home details and other stuff. We were pointed to a hotel a hundred or so yards away were we could ring for a taxi as the ski buses had long since stopped running. I thanked our rescuers sincerely, and they were all happy to shake hands with me.

The guy in charge told me we would never have made it down the piste without skis. He also told me we would not have survived the night in the open. We perhaps then owe our lives to an unknown German skier. A short time later we were in a warm taxi heading back to our hotel.

We never saw Dave again; he left for an early plane at Verona airport, before we were up and about. After a late breakfast Andrew and I returned our skiing gear, and had a last look around the charming village before we too left for out flight home. Verona airport was fog bound – we had to be bussed to Venice. I can at least say I have been to Venice.

Andrew got married, and I subsequently took my youngest daughter skiing to Hoch-Gurgl in Austria two years running, she was also a quick learner, and was soon skiing very well. A couple of years later the four of us went skiing to Kaprun in Austria. Shortly after we were there they had that awful tragedy in Kaprun, when the train caught fire in the tunnel going up the mountain, with terrible loss of life. We had been using that same train for seven days. I actually did get to ski a black run in Hoch-Gurgl, but I made sure I was on my own.

PS. Before we left the rescue team, I asked the leader what we could have done differently. He replied, 'I don't know – you were lucky.'

The Traveller

The traveller looked out of place
As he walked along the way.
People were asking who he was,
But he wasn't going to say.

His appearance was unusual;
Flowing gown – determined pace,
His eyes didn't stray from the road ahead;
And he had this certain grace.

A few people now had gathered,
But didn't try to get too near;
They just followed on in silence,
There was just a hint of fear.

When the market place came into view,
He began to slow his pace,
Slowly now, he looked around;
Pure innocence on his face.

As he turned to meet the crowd;
A young woman struggled through,
Her hands before – as if in prayer;
She alone knew what was true.

She ran up to the traveller,
Arms twined in warm embrace,
And as she held him tenderly;
A tear ran down her face.

A policeman now came into view,
Attracted by the crowd,
He didn't try to interfere,
But stepped back with head bowed.

The lady took the offered hand,
On this special day;
The silent crowd then parted,
And the Son was led away.

'You must not go out on your own,
It's not safe for you, or me,'
His answer was an angelic smile;
Her son was only three.

Potency – can you grasp it?

I felt a potency out there
It's true I swear it's true
I felt it all around me
And was not sure what to do.
This isn't just a recent thing
I have known it for a while
It's very hard to nail it down
But it certainly has style.
My eyes were first to be aware
But there was nothing I could see
And then my ears detected it
But no sounds came to me.
My nose was next to tell me
I knew I was not wrong
But strangely though, there was no smell
What on earth was going on?
My tongue then sent a message
But no taste at all came through
This was not imagination
Everything – I knew was true.
But then I stretched my arms out
And grasped the air around
It was then I knew I had it
The strength at last I'd found.
So if you're feeling low and sad
Your problems you must share –
Throw your arms out wide and grasp it
There is potency out there!

Tommy and the Tin

Tommy set out from his home for his Saturday morning shopping trip. This was a weekly event and there was little deviation. He was eighty-four years old, slightly stooped now with the ravages of advancing years, his hair was grey and thinning but he never wore a hat. He was always clean, but still looked a little tatty. The fawn coloured raincoat, which he obviously favoured, was the worse for wear; his shoes had long since lost their shine; he walked with a pronounced limp using a stick. Why the local kids jeered and taunted him he never knew. He only thought, 'Well they are only kids, what do they know?'

He caught the ten-forty-five bus, and the twenty-minute ride took him nearly to the local supermarket. This particular morning just before entering the shop a very smart, immaculately-dressed gentleman approached him. They spoke for a few minutes, and Tommy then carried on into the shop. The whole trip took just over ninety minutes and found Tommy walking back up his street with a number of supermarket bags. If the children were about he would have to endure the jibes again. He never was offered a hand to carry his bags.

After Tommy had entered his kitchen and put his purchases away he put the kettle on and made himself a pot of tea. He took the tea into the living room and placed it on his table, placed his coat over a chair and sat down. While sipping his tea his eyes were drawn to an old tin which had pride of place on his old sideboard. He never took his eyes from the tin until he had emptied his cup, then he went over and picked it up. He seemed to be having an internal battle whether to open it or not. After a few minutes he levered up the lid of the old tin. One at a time he removed five medals. The medals were dull and tarnished, the ribbons were tatty and faded. Tommy didn't seem to notice this. He took the medals to the coat he had just removed and pinned them one by one, in no particular order or neatness, to the left-hand side.

Tommy was in France the day after the invasion. His job as a driver was to shuttle between the front line and the field hospitals with the wounded soldiers. It was on one such trip whilst loading his truck which had been hastily converted to carry the injured, that he became the target for a German machine-gunner. The German soldier was only about twenty yards away. A Bren-gun carrier quickly took out the enemy machine gunner. Tommy drove his truck back and delivered his wounded charges to the field hospital before he collapsed unconscious. He had received eight hits. Three had passed through but five bullets were still in him. Tommy woke up in an English

Military hospital. He gradually recovered and papers were prepared for his discharge. He objected to this and pleaded to see the war out. His plea was accepted and he was promised light duties. He spent a short time in Northern Ireland driving military personnel in light vehicles, but not long after he was posted back to France. He found himself once more driving heavy trucks including tank transporters to the front line for the American troops. He survived the war without any more injuries.

The next morning, Sunday, a smart car arrived outside Tommy's house. A driver in military uniform escorted Tommy to the car. Tommy had the same clothes that he'd worn for the supermarket visit; this time however he also had his five medals hanging from his coat.

The car stopped at the war memorial just beside the church. Tommy was helped out of the car and gently guided to his spot.

During the previous few weeks the Royal British Legion had been looking for a local man to lay the first tribute at the remembrance service. Someone had stumbled across Tommy's war record and he was contacted. At first he declined, but after some gentle persuasion he accepted. He was presented with a Royal Corps of Transport beret and badge for the occasion – his old regiment. After the two-minute silence, Tommy put his beret on. An army captain walked up to Tommy and saluted him. Tommy saluted back. Tommy took the offered floral tribute. He placed his stick on the ground and walked the nine or ten yards to the memorial. He carefully laid the tribute on the base, stood up as straight as he could and then saluted the memorial. Tears were clearly seen running down his cheeks and he took a grubby hanky from his pocked and dabbed at his face. He stood stationary in the total silence for about a minute. Looking around it was easy to see other cheeks being dabbed and I think some of the cheeks were of children. Tommy eventually stepped back a yard and saluted again. He then turned and walked back to his position. The Salvation Army band then played a medley of marches as the remaining dignitaries, and others laid their tributes.

After the ceremony was over Tommy was quite the celebrity. Many of the contingents from the three services were anxious to talk to him, and he seemed to be quite happy chatting to them all. Tommy was driven back home and escorted back to his door. After taking off his raincoat he carefully removed the medals from his coat. He then placed them in the tin and secured the lid. The tin was then placed back on his sideboard. The beret was placed at the side of the tin with its gleaming badge pointing outwards. Tommy had had his moment of glory; he knew that he wouldn't be wearing the beret again, or levering that lid from the battered Andrews Liver Salts tin again either.

In an English Country Garden

Why don't you feed your own things,
You folk of Pateley Bridge?
You seem to leave it all to us,
From animal to midge.
There is every kind of living thing,
On the ground and in the air
No matter how we feed them,
They all return and stare.
There are jackdaws, crows, and magpies,
With small birds by the score.
Ducks and geese and pigeons,
They must think we own a store.
These birds are all unfillable;
We feel that we get stung!
'Cos when they've eaten all our food,
They come back with their young.
The squirrels are insatiable
And soon get in a rage,
They not only eat the seed and nuts;
They eat the bloody cage.
There're rabbits bobbing all around.
And hedgehogs call by too.
We've even got some foxes,
I swear to you-it's true.
We feel we're feeding everything,
Even the one's just passing by,
And early every morning
There is such a hue and cry.
So come on you folk of Pateley,
We're really not that posh!
Please start to feed your own things,
Then we can save some *DOSH*.

The Arrival of Godot

This is my take on what the third act, of the two - act play by Samuel Beckett may have been like. Godot actually turns up...

You will need a passing acquaintance of the said play to fully appreciate the following.

The scene opens with two tramps waking up and stretching beneath a leafless tree.

Estra: Good morning Vlad.
Vlad: Morning Estra.
Estra: Sleep well?
Vlad: Not bad, about two hours.
Estra: Well that's a good percentage.
Vlad: Percentage of what?
Estra: Percentage of more hours.
Vlad: Oh, I see what you mean.
Estra: (Looking around) Have you eaten?
Vlad: (Also looking around) Eaten what?
Estra: Eaten breakfast.
Vlad: Oh that, no.
Estra: Why?
Vlad: Nothing to eat.
Estra: I still have this black radish.
Vlad: I only like pink radishes.
Vlad: Yes you are right, who wants a black radish?
Estra: (Looking down the road) Well, he never came.
Vlad: Who never came?
Estra: Godot
Vlad: Who is Godot?
Estra: The guy we were waiting for.
Vlad: Oh, him. Why didn't he come?
Estra: Maybe he was busy.
Vlad: (Looking pensively around) Maybe we missed him.
Estra: I haven't missed him – I never met him.
Vlad: (Looking down the road) Let's go.
Estra: Go where – where can we go?
Vlad: (Now looking down at the ground) We can't, can we?
Estra: Why?

Vlad: (In a quiet voice) Because we are waiting for Godot.
Estra: But he isn't coming.
Vlad: Why?
Estra: Well he hasn't come yet.
Vlad: He may have been busy.
Estra: But he let us down twice.
Vlad: Well what's twice?
Estra: It's a fair percentage.
Vlad: (Looking down the road again) I can get some breakfast for a shilling.
Estra: You said it was more.
Vlad: We can save a penny today.
Estra: But at what cost?
Vlad: (Pausing to think about the answer before speaking) Anyway we can't go.
Estra: Why?
Vlad: Somebody has to wait for Godot.
Estra: (With hand up to eye) Can you see someone up the road?
Vlad: It might be the two who were here yesterday.
Estra: (Looking puzzled) I thought they were just a dream.
Vlad: Well yes they might have been.
Estra: (Now clearly agitated) He's getting nearer.
Vlad: Do you think it is Godot?
Estra: If it was we wouldn't be waiting anymore.
Vlad: What would we do then?
Estra: We could wait for someone else.
Vlad: But it wouldn't be the same.
Estra: (Looking puzzled again) Same as what?
Vlad: Same as waiting for Godot.
Estra: Yes, you are right.
Vlad: Can you see if it is Godot?
Estra: I have never seen Godot. What does he look like?
Vlad: You have a good point.
Estra: Can you see what he looks like?
Vlad: Yes, he looks like Godot.
Estra: (Looking anxiously) Tidy up your hat and let us sit under the tree.
Vlad: Don't say anything about hanging.
Estra: Or Boots –
Vlad: Or trousers –
Estra: (Obviously thinking hard) But Godot will know about those things anyway. He knows everything
Vlad: I know that but don't tell him just in case.

(a man appears, it is Godot)

Estra: Good morning to you sir.
Godot: Good morning.
Vlad: Good morning to you sir.
Godot: Good morning. Been here long?
Vlad: No, just two days.
Estra: Two days, that's a fair percentage.
Vlad: Well now you're here can we go?
Godot: Go where?
Estra: Well anywhere – we are fed up of this tree.
Godot: But it is a good place to wait.
Vlad: Wait for what?
Godot: Wait for anything.
Estra: What have you to wait for?
Godot: There are two.
Vlad: Two what?
Godot: (Looking from Vlad to Estra and back to Vlad) Well I think there should be two? Maybe there is just one. Someone I am to meet here today.
Vlad: (The situation slowly dawning and looking enquiringly at Estra) Did we get it wrong? Did we get here two days early?
Estra: (With total confusion on his face) Well it's a fair percentage. (And then quietly) What's to be done?
Vlad/Estra: (Both now looking at each other, then slowly turning to look at Godot say together) Let's Go.

(Nobody moves)

Curtain slowly falls.

Choices

I wouldn't mind being a bird,
Soaring way up in the sky.
With their super colours and shapes;
And oh to be able to fly.
I wouldn't mind being a tree,
Standing proud in some safe wood;
With my mighty branches, protecting the earth,
Yes! I'd be a tree if I could.
I wouldn't mind being an insect,
Industrious all night, and all day;
Working below and above ground,
I wonder if they ever play?
I wouldn't mind being a flower,
With such lovely colours and smell,
With bees dropping in for refreshment;
O' my, I could do that so well.
I wouldn't mind being a river,
Unpolluted, so wide and so deep;
Meandering slow through the country,
With all the life safe in my keep.
I wouldn't mind being a mountain,
So vast, so majestic and tall;
The nearest thing to heaven is a mountain,
I just wouldn't mind that at all.
But I don't want to be a fox,
A whale or a tiger or bear;
But most of all, not a human being;
Because they just destroy, and don't care.

Tommy's Funeral

The Good Lord giveth and the Lord will take.'
'Are they sultanas in that cake?'
'We remember Tommy in the war.'
'Sausage rolls were great, going back for some more.'
The church is full, 'Are they apple pies?'
And lots of hankies up to eyes.
Tommy was neglected, did anyone care?
Then at his funeral – they're all bloody there.
Eulogies galore – 'Was like a father to me,
The bravest man you would ever see.'
'The worlds a worst place now,' one said with a grin.
'Did you see the medals he kept in his tin?'
'I remember Dunkirk with so many dead.'
'Is that garlic I smell on the bread?'
'Yes Tommy got shot there.' – the ham sandwich was poked,
'Indeed badly wounded – is that salmon smoked?'
If Tommy could have seen this crowd
He surely would have screamed out loud
He'd never seen them all for years
Now milling round with all those tears.
Where were they when he'd cried all day?
Always too busy – or too far away.
'Look at them all – just here for the tea
None of them gave a jot about me.'
'The day though gavest Lord is ended
The darkness falls at thy behest,'
'This apple pie is really nice,
Old Tommy always liked the best.'
'Well poor Tommy's left us all for good,
I didn't realise he was ill –
We must all promise now to keep in touch.'
'Yes indeed, I'm sure we will ....'

The Lecture

This was the chance I had been waiting for, to join this exclusive club. Many had tried, but few had succeeded. It had come as quite a surprise when the envelope had been brought to my door by a private messenger.

I had to present myself at the venue at a certain time with my prepared lecture. I would be giving a short introduction, then it would be straight into the lecture with a guarantee of no interruptions. They held over the right to question me at the end if they felt it justified. I had been given a small list of subjects which I could lecture on. I would have preferred to have chosen my own subject but this wasn't to be.

When I arrived I was taken straight to the podium, given a few moments to prepare myself, and then asked to give my introduction. Before starting I looked out at the eminent group sitting before me. There were perhaps fifty members in the hall. I deliberately made eye-contact with some, and then gave my brief introduction. Two minutes later and without any ado I started my lecture which I hoped fitted in okay with the strict time allowance I had been given.

'Gentlemen I ask you to consider this – Albert Einstein was quoted as saying "The man who thinks his life is meaningless is not only unhappy but hardly fit for life at all". He also stated that "The more life progresses the less room there seems to be for a God". It was Sigmund Freud who taught that God was an illusion. People who deny God, however, can offer no explanation for the complex biological design. Darwin tells how he thinks life developed but could not offer any idea how it started. Many people reject God because of the awful suffering they see around them – "How could God allow this to happen?". Many would never believe in God if they met him – they want to live their lives their way without any interference. Still we have to accept that many people keep looking for a purpose and a meaning.

'We live in an expanding universe of that there is no doubt. We know then that there had to be a beginning.

'"A beginning of what?" would be a good question. Well consider that our Earth would fit into our sun over a million times; that our sun is only one of millions in our galaxy; that it would take light 100,000 years to cross it; that our galaxy is just a minute part of the universe, and each of these other galaxies have billions of stars which are all in order, all in motion. Could this possibly be the result of some huge indiscriminate explosion?

'We are led to believe by scientists that everything started with a small dot – a singularity. Well okay but where did this awesome singularity which caused this vast universe come from? I think it was Bernard Lovell who said, "We have to face the problem of a beginning". He went on to state that if the universe had expanded one million-millionth part faster, our universe would have dispersed by now. He also held that if it had expanded more slowly, then gravitational forces would have caused the universe to collapse early on in its life.

'What about this order? I hear you ask. Well let us look at the electromagnetic force to start with. If this force was significantly weaker, electrons would not be held by the atom with a result that atoms could not then form molecules. On the other hand if this force was just a little stronger, electrons would be trapped at the nucleus of the atom. This would mean no chemical reactions and in either case this means no life. If the electromagnetic force was slightly lower, gravity would be lower, and this would result in smaller stars as their internal temperatures would not then be high enough to cause nuclear fusion – the sun would not (could not) shine. If gravity was slightly higher, stars including our sun would find their life expectancy greatly reduced. The question then has to be: is this design or chance?'

I had to wait quite a long time after my application to the Society before I received the invitation to present a talk. I knew the reason for this was for them to do a detailed background check. I had no problems with that. The problem I had was when I saw the three subjects which had been selected. The subjects are changed for each new applicant apparently so there is no possibility of lecture by memory. I had three days to prepare.

The first subject was 'On the evolution of the human eye'. It did not take me long to dismiss this one. I know that arguments have raged over this subject. I have of course had an interest: it is a fascinating subject. It is also a subject were one could come to disaster very quickly when talking to people who couldn't be fooled. One would only have to go off on the wrong tangent and while the lecture might be commendable, you could fail miserably. No – that one was out.

The second subject was 'On the frontal Lobe'. Now this was better, there being plenty of scope here. However after a little thought I realised I would just be quoting facts that had been investigated by others over many years; there would be nothing I could add personally, and no matter how well I presented the talk, I knew it would not be good enough. I realised that this was the 'stooge' subject and I was grateful that I had spotted it.

The last subject, 'On Accident or Design', was the one I would go for. This was a subject that had fascinated me for years, and one that I knew I could talk about without any trouble. My memory is poor these days but I knew that plenty of facts were available and the subject offered much scope. The problem was the time limit given for the lecture. It would have to be condensed and the most important bits included. I would not try to influence one way or the other so could not fail on that score.

Observations in C Major – 119

'Excuse me for a moment, gentlemen.' I had stopped to have a drink of water and to relax for a few seconds. This was perfectly normal and acceptable during a lecture, and I used the short break to gain eye contact with a few more members of the group before continuing.

At this point I went quite deeply into a few physics effects. It is not my intention to bore you with theory; however I will give a very simple explanation as it is very important part of the lecture. I went on to discuss the 'strong nuclear force'. Very briefly this force glues protons and neutrons together in the nucleus of the atom. This bonding is responsible for all our elements. It seems that if this force was only two percent weaker only hydrogen would exist. If the binding force was slightly stronger no hydrogen would be found. No hydrogen means no water or food, and the sun would not function. I then discussed the 'weak nuclear force' – this force is critical because it allows our sun to burn at just the correct rate. This controlled burn gives us life; without the force we would incinerate. I then asked my audience (not expecting a reply at this time) if this fine tuning was by accident or design.

Noticing that my amber light was blinking and I had just thirty seconds to wind down, I finished bang on the dot.

There was no obvious reaction from the group before me – after a few seconds a gentleman stood up and asked me to relax for a few minutes.

This gentleman then went round his colleagues, who were now in small clusters, and exchanged words. He then approached me and told me I could have two minutes to describe how I thought my lecture had been received, and then I would be asked some questions, so again I took my place on the podium.

'Gentlemen, I would like to think that my lecture could have been presented anywhere and understood. I deliberately tried to keep it interesting and understandable. I know that you gentlemen are aware that a lecture on this subject could take a whole day and still not cover all the points. It was my intention to raise just a few of the many points – well enough to possibly start a good discussion.'

The guy who seemed to be in charge of proceedings then told me they had just two questions. I was relieved to hear there were to be only two.

'Here is our first question. What is the significance of the Earth's distance from the sun?'

After about ten seconds I answered, 'Gentlemen our earth is just the right size for our existence. If the earth was only slightly larger, gravity would be stronger and hydrogen would collect – being unable to escape the increase in gravity, this factor would render the earth unsuitable for life. If the earth were slightly smaller our life-sustaining oxygen would escape and surface water would evaporate. In either scenario, life would not be possible. The earth's distance from the sun is the most amazing thing. Studies of the ratio of the earth's radius and distance from the sun concluded that human life would not be possible if the earth had been just five percent nearer the sun, because of overheating. If we had been placed just one percent further away from the sun, runaway ice covering would have occurred thousands of years ago. The earth also rotates at just the right speed to maintain comfortable temperatures. Were this speed faster or slower the extremes in temperature would mean life was impossible. These factors would appear to have been calculated very carefully.'

'Thank you. Here is our final question. How does the second law of thermodynamics fit in here?'

Again I needed a few seconds to reply, they were clearly testing my immediate knowledge. I answered, 'If you bought a new building and a new car and left both alone, the building would become a ruin and the car a wreck. This law applies to the universe also, but there we see order constantly maintained. The study of entropy or orderliness of our observable universe shows it to be unchanged. Who is maintaining it?'

'We take that to mean that you are for design then?'

I wasn't expecting this question, and they knew it – all eyes were on me.

I didn't know what their thoughts were and I certainly wasn't going to compromise myself anyway, so I answered, 'Gentlemen, I would most definitely have to come down on the side of design. It is my opinion that we are not here through accident.'

'We wish to thank you for your lecture, please be seated for a while.'

The jury now departed into an adjoining room, and very soon afterwards a charming young lady entered from another door and offered me tea or coffee. Whist drinking my coffee the young lady told me that the decision on my application for membership would take a while, and would be delivered to me privately. She wished me good luck as I left the building a few minutes later.

It took three weeks for the envelope to arrive by private courier. It had a distinguished emblem on the front. There was no mistaking where it was from. It took me a while before I had the courage to open it.

Twenty-Two

This poem was written to commemorate a young lady's 22nd birthday, on the island of Tenerife in the year 1990

The gold no longer shines so bright,
Owls no longer fly at night.
Most animals have ceased to be,
There are no fish now in the sea.

The snow and ice fight hard to stay,
But the rays of the sun are stronger today.
Waterfalls all dried up now,
Milk no more comes from the cow.
The snake no longer tries to hiss,
Our children aren't allowed to kiss.
Criminals are walking free,
The prisoners now, are you and me.
Aeroplanes no longer fly,
The elderly refuse to die.
These prophesies are coming true
The warning's clear to all of you.
There may still be time to put things right,
But the gold no longer shines so bright.

The Painter

Grim are the faces now drifting about
The shadow's they cast are much fainter –
The carpenter has long since left
Maybe now it is time for the painter.
Surely the painter has got things right
Cover the scratch and mistake,
Finish off with a nice bright gloss
No need to apply that brake –
So speed along – having no care
Enjoy all the wonder and fun.
Just keep painting over those cracks
Then look back at the things you have done.
So, feeling proud, done quite well?
Maybe life has treated you grand,
But you're marked my friend; there is no escape
You still have some paint on your hand –

Tracy's Letter

Somebody told me that the Vicar had appealed in the church magazine for fresh contributors. It seems the same people write it every month. I can well understand his request; it must be one boring magazine. Anyway in response to that request I thought I would tell you a little about my friend Sandra.

Some time ago Sandra presented herself to the local general hospital casualty department. She had a very bad chest. Well okay, admittedly she smokes forty fags a day, but her GP was not too nice to her on her frequent visits to see him; all he did was tell her to stop smoking. Sandra just wanted her cough making better not to stop bloody smoking. She thought they might be more helpful at the hospital hence her visit. Whilst she was waiting (and this was a long time, because she was not considered an urgent case) a woman rushed in with a boy who was bleeding badly. Well, Sandra is a sensitive girl, and cannot stand the sight of blood. In fact it screwed her right up – and she had to leave the hospital very quickly without receiving any treatment.

Sandra had a girl friend, who knew a girl who is a solicitor. It was quickly established that because of the trauma she had suffered, she should sue the hospital for being irresponsible. It was considered she should not have been subjected to the distressing sight of blood in the hospital. Sandra didn't work, so legal aid was obtained. To cut a long story short, the judge, on summing up the case, said that the hospital was totally irresponsible. People should be able to visit hospitals without being subject to the sight of blood, even in casualty departments. She stated that people with injuries that are bleeding, should consider other people before rushing into hospitals.

The judge said that Sandra being a sensitive soul must have suffered enormously from her ordeal. How could she ever rise to be a leader in commerce, become a captain of a battleship, a jet fighter pilot, or even become a High Court judge like herself. She agreed Sandra's working life had been ruined (that bit was strange because she has never worked) and awarded her two million pounds. The hospital had to pay – they dare not risk anymore expense. Well, it wasn't going to be that simple for Sandra. She took lots of holidays all over the world; she had new cars every month, and changed houses frequently. Her latest house has a tennis court and swimming pool, but as you can imagine – she is still suffering.

Because of irresponsible men, Sandra found herself with three children by three different fathers at a very young age, and because of her trauma at the hospital she cannot bring herself to visit them now (not that she ever went much before). I know what she is feeling like though – irresponsible men left me with three kids. They are also in care, but I do try to visit them once or twice a year. The worst thing is, and this is nasty: when on holiday in Africa, Sandra got friendly with some guys (she was always a friendly girl) and now finds she has a nasty disease. The doctor told her it was her own fault, and that her problem was self-induced but Sandra couldn't agree – she insisted it was the bloody Africans who caused it. Men are so irresponsible. I totally agree with Sandra here, men should be abolished, they are just so selfish and useless.

I was lying in bed with Sandra the other morning having a fag and a gin, watching the telly, when this idiot came on asking for more money to go to things like Parkinson's, Alzheimer's, and Arthritis research – what a bloody fool, we'd never heard of them, well, hardly ever. We know where the money should go to, and it's not to bloody silly things like that. What a waste of our money, we both thought. After this medical idiot, a bloody religious idiot came on, okay admittedly we'd had a few more gins, but this guy was a complete nutter. He was trying to raise money for Christian Aid, well okay if that is where you want your money to go, but Sandra and me have never had any bloody Christian Aid so why should we give any of ours?

You religious types are okay, well some of you, but just leave us alone. 'Money doesn't grow on bloody trees' Sandra said, and I have to agree with her there.

Anyway we flicked through the channels and found a 'triangle film' that's much more in our line. It's nice watching a good X-rated in bed with a few fags and a nice drinky. Since Sandra's trauma she has had to buy illegal drugs to preserve her sanity, her doctor will not prescribe them. I had to join her of course; I couldn't let her take them on her own – so we are both completely screwed up now.

This whole business today is about responsibility, and not many people have any. When Sandra was awarded her money, I decided to befriend her in her time of need. Now that was a responsible act. We have both really tried to act reasonably, but unfortunately we found ourselves surrounded by spongers and hangers on who just wanted something for bloody nothing. Me and Sandra can't stand people like that; some bloody people don't half have a cheek. Thank goodness there are still people like Sandra's solicitor and the judge about, who are sensible and caring. The solicitor and judge in Sandra's case were both feminists, same as Sandra and me.

Well, I will leave you now. I suppose this article will be very different to the usual rubbish that you read in the church magazine, but remember you asked for it! I will let you know how Sandra is getting on sometime, if you like.

Tracy. X

PS. Sandra has just told me she thinks she is preggers again; what a bloody card that one is. She is not bothered though, 'cos she likes kids.

Phthalo Blue

We shared our hopes and thoughts it's true
There were so many things that we would do.
But destiny had its part to play,
The forever blue was turning grey
Years have flown, toll has been paid,
Routes planned out, and pathways laid;
The forever blue that some now see,
Still seems quite dark and grey to me.
Life's journey is only leased that's true –
Please take the grey and return the blue.
Our search for pleasure is never done,
Just who is the selfish one?
So unlock the door – throw away the key
And then perchance some blue we'll see.
And in the seasons of my mind –
I pray for all, the blue we find.
All the hopes and thoughts, I shared with you
I return with love – wrapped in Phthalo Blue.

Musica et Lacrima

Musical composition is not just for the likes of Mozart, Wagner, Elgar *et al*. Believe me, it is possible for anybody to compose. It is not overly difficult. Maybe I had a head start because I have always loved classical music, but it is within the reach of anyone capable of creating a tune in their heads. I must tell you now that I have never had any musical training. I would have dearly loved to have had the opportunity to learn the piano, however being brought up during a war, with everything in turmoil, it was not possible.

We didn't have music lessons at school in those days, so I left school with no knowledge of music whatsoever. Since then throughout my working life I have come to love music, mainly classical. I always seemed to have a tune in my head, and it was about six years ago, that I began to think that maybe I could somehow get the music down on paper. Delius managed this in his later life of course when he was no longer able to write; he had a friend as his amanuensis, one Eric Fenby. He wrote some tremendous music with this arrangement. Some other well-known composers have used this method of composition, including Liszt, Handel and Mozart. Unfortunately there was to be no amanuensis for me.

Nevertheless I persisted. I knew of musical notes as letters – I suppose everyone knows that much. It occurred to me that if I could transpose the letter notation into musical notation, I could be nearly there. So off to the library I went and found a book on musical theory and notation. This book told me everything that I needed to know, note lengths, speed, how to denote level of sound, etc.

Now I needed a keyboard. To start with I bought a simple Yamaha, some manuscript paper and waited for inspiration. My inspiration always came when I was walking our dog first thing in the morning. I used to go over the fields, and compose in my head. On return I was straight to my cassette recorder to get my opus down on tape. So far so good, at this stage any decent amanuensis could have taken over but I am afraid it was to be the hard route for me. After work and evening meal, my musical work would start, first getting the audio down into letter notation. With the help of the keyboard this was relatively easy. It got more difficult changing the letter notation into musical notation, but I did it. I didn't know what key my music was in until I finished transposing it. I taught myself to play the keyboard, well enough to be able to play my compositions.

Next I had to find out if a musician could understand and play what I had written. The first two people I approached – both church organists – didn't want to know. They were patronising. I am sure they thought I was an idiot. However one Sunday morning our normal organist was not at church and a young man from London was playing. He was on holiday and it had been arranged that he could play for us. This guy was amazing. He produced sounds we had never heard before. After the service, instead of leaving the church, everyone stayed seated to hear his final piece. Then, quite unusual in a church, there was spontaneous applause. I said to my wife, 'That's the guy who will play my music.' She told me not to be silly, and didn't want me to ask him. I couldn't see a problem, so when the guy who I now know as Trevor Dawson finished at the organ, I went up to him introduced myself. I told him how brilliant he was – then hit him with my request. Trevor said he would be delighted to help, we arranged to meet in church the following Tuesday. I brought some recording equipment. My eldest daughter came along to help with the recording. We finished setting up then waited in anticipation. I was just doing a bit of improvisation on the organ checking the sound levels when Trevor walked in. I presented him with my music, which he had not seen before. Remember this music had not been written for church organ, so Trevor had to add the appropriate chords and pedal details. After about ten minutes we were ready to go.

I had given him four pieces to play. We did them one at a time. Unfortunately the primary recording system overloaded and was distorted, however we were running a secondary system and so captured the recordings reasonably well. I couldn't believe what I had on tape. Trevor's interpretation of my music was superb.

My mother died shortly after this recording, and this music was played as the introit and recessional music at her funeral. I subsequently went on to write a wedding march for my youngest daughter.

Now, walking down the aisle with a beautiful daughter on one's arm is moving enough, but when the organist bursts forth with the wedding march that you have composed? – I was destroyed. When we arrived at the altar my face was wet with tears. I don't know if the vicar's glance at me was one of shame or pity. I managed to compose myself until the first hymn. Certain hymns have a devastating effect on me under normal conditions. Why I chose the three hymns that always screwed me up I still don't know – but I did, and they did. More strange glances from the vicar. I chose Jerusalem for the recessional march. This music completely destroys me – another big mistake. I had a very soggy hankie.

Towards the end of the service the vicar made an announcement that I had written the introit wedding march and I had to stand for a round of applause. My daughter still has me on about this and has me laughing – she says I must be the only father to receive applause at his daughter's wedding.

Later, at the reception, things returned to normal. But when I reached into my sporran for the notes for my speech – of course, they were missing.

If only I could afford an amanuensis.

Perception

Jealousy Envy and Perception met
As they were wont to do.
They talked about their successes
And who they had managed to screw.
They were aware of their mighty power,
And how people used their skill –
Being utilised more and more,
They just loved being used for the kill.
But this time they had an argument –
Jealousy claimed he was the top spot
The root of most of the evil around
But the other two said that was just rot.
Envy, then let them both know where he stood
Surely he was the worst of the three,
He had the power to destroy at a stroke,
Yes he was top, it was so plain to see.
Then it was Perception's turn –
He stood and looked round very dour;
You two fade into insignificance
When compared to my mighty power.
I am the cause of most problems;
I destroy folks by the hour and day.
People use me instead of stopping to think,
It's so much easier that way.
So convenient to get the wrong idea,
And make one's self feel fine.
It's such a doddle and doesn't take any effort,
To fall back on ways like mine.
People don't have to use their brains;
I'm happy to do all the graft
It's all so easy when I'm about,
And folk's just love using my craft.
They don't need to employ any effort at all,
Please remember I do everything free
So if you're in doubt, just alter your views,
And be always right just like me.

You won't need facts or any proof,
When it's me you set out to employ
I'm the bringer of grief, tears and sorrow,
And the destroyer of any joy.
People lose all their reason when I am around,
It's the option that's so easy to use
Folks seldom try with my nice side,
It's the high ground that makes people bruise.
So I claim the title of worst –
The worst word that's ever been.
And jealousy and envy just stood open mouthed
But their faces had turned a bright green ….

Endorphins

Strange things can happen when one is under stress. When I was training for distance running, I used to put myself under tremendous physical stress. Many people have experienced weird things while in this state, not just me.

What happens apparently is that under prolonged physical stress the brain is prompted to go into overproduction of endorphins. Endorphins are a natural group of peptide neurotransmitters occurring in the brain. These under normal conditions can produce pain relief and soporific effects. However under prolonged physical stress some funny things can happen.

During my training I ran many miles on my own, but on some occasions I also ran with colleagues. From conversations I had, I began to realize that I was not alone in experiencing strange effects, although I soon found out that my experience was somewhat different to my companions.

One of my running friends was a medical doctor, and he was the first person that I spoke to about my experience. Two of my friends had had their own. One of them used to experience a floating action – this happened on a hard run, probably seven-minute miles, at maybe ten miles. He described it as running on air. It didn't happen every time, but was frequent. Another found his memory increased dramatically during this period. There are other effects that people have experienced.

What happened to me was totally different and I have never heard of anyone else having this same phenomenon. My colour perception increased. It was the weirdest thing, and I was glad to be able to relate it to my doctor friend. He had not heard of this particular one before, was very interested in it, but not overly concerned as the brain can do very funny things when under stress.

The strange thing was that it stayed increased sometimes for hours. When I returned from training runs, instead of going straight for a shower I used to go and look at flowers! I saw the most intense colours and shades; it would not be possible for me to describe them.

When my marathon running came to an end, so did my hard training sessions. Although I do not experience the same intensity of colour again, I am convinced I still have a high colour perception and indeed still spend long periods just looking at coloured objects. They fascinate me. I have studied colour theory in depth during my professional life, but cannot find any reason why my colour acuity was enhanced, and apparently stayed that way, other than by physical stress. The answer seems to be the morphiate-type substance produced under physical stress which gives a 'high' and produces strange effects. I have never taken any drugs other than the odd pain-relief tablet, but I understand that these results are not entirely dissimilar to effects described from people who do take drugs. Maybe the answer to drug takers is to take up running instead. You may still get the high – and you will be a darn sight fitter!

A Badge Too Far

Change his clothes and wash his head
Remove bananas from his bed.
Pick his teeth up from the floor
Scrape his dinner from the drawer

Laid on bed with mournful stare
Not knowing what, or why or where.
Just the same as yesterday
I'm sure he'd like to fade away.

Things were different in the war
Fighting on an Eastern shore
No memories of that time now
No memories, of when or how.

Wash his face and shave his chin
Find his teeth and put them in
Hold his hand and say I care
All I get back is that stare.

I talk to him about times of fun –
When we strolled beneath an Indian sun
Sometimes a nod as I hold his hand
Does he really understand?

No memory of family past
Of eleven he was the last.
Royal telegram for sixty years –
But for his wife he sheds no tears.

I am his only child you see
And my dad just doesn't know it's me
I talk to him but does he hear?
Does he know his daughter's near?

*His veteran's badge arrived today
For the six years he was away
I'll go to him and pin it on
Remembering times when he was strong.*

The citation:

With the compliments of the Under Secretary of State for Defence and Minister for Veterans. This HM Armed Forces Veteran's Badge is presented to you in recognition of your service to your country.

Ministry of Defence, Whitehall.

Incident on a Caribbean Reef

We had had a wonderful few days lounging in the sun on the wonderful sands, eating coconuts straight from the trees along with other exotic fruits. This place was truly a tropical paradise. It was about halfway through the week when I asked my wife if she fancied snorkelling on the reef. I had snorkelled in the lagoon quite a bit and it was quite an amazing experience.

Shirley, my wife, is not a strong swimmer and was a bit reluctant – the reef being about one mile out. She agreed to the boat ride out, but reserved judgment on the diving until we were out at the reef. I booked us on the boat for the following afternoon. There were about twenty people on the boat and we slowly made our way out to the drop-off point where we were kitted out with life jackets and snorkelling gear. Shirley took a little time to be tempted into the water – but she eventually decided to give it a try. This area surpassed all the sights I had viewed in the lagoon; the variation of sea creatures and the fantastic coral varieties were truly breathtaking. Shirley soon got into the swing of things and thoroughly enjoyed the experience as did all the others present.

I think we had about forty-five minutes on the reef, then we were called back to the boat. We removed our gear and it was stashed away. With our towels wrapped round us, we headed back to shore, all eager to relate our experiences about the wonders we had just been privileged to see. We were nearly back to the beach when someone said, 'Where is the lady who was on her own'. There were ten couples and one single lady when we set off to the reef – the single lady had not been checked back on the boat.

It was now starting to get dusk and the boat was quickly turned around. This was no speedboat, it was just a flat-bottomed reef boat – very slow. It seemed to take an age to retrace our path back to the reef. Eventually we arrived at roughly the same spot and started shouting for the lady. There was no reply. We all knew how easy it was to drift away from the boat, we were told to always make sure we didn't lose sight of it. Even so, it had been hard to swim back on occasions. I had stayed very close to Shirley all the time we were in the water.

Panic was now starting to set in among the boat crew and also amongst us. It was a frightening scenario. Sharks were known to visit these parts. There were sting rays, barracuda, snakes and other dangerous creatures which would not bother groups of people but would not be frightened by a lone swimmer. It was decided to circle our original diving spot and slowly increase our circle, hoping to come across the lady. I always maintain we should have continued to the beach and reported the situation, but I was overruled by the crew who obviously didn't want anyone to know we had left a swimmer on the reef.

We were now in serious trouble. The sea had also developed quite a swell. It was on our third sweep and quite a long way from our original spot when we found the lady. She had been swept a fair distance out. She had soon realised that swimming back was not an option and decided very sensibly to float on the water and keep still. She was one very frightened and lucky person. On the boat she soon recovered, but couldn't understand how we could have gone without her. It was of course the crew's job to count the people back on board. If that astute passenger hadn't noticed the lady was missing I am sure no one else would have. It could easily have been a disaster.

This incident happened in the Dominican Republic in 1990. Shirley and I often recall it, and the wonderful holiday we had. I was prompted to write this account after recently reading about a similar incident where a couple were left behind.

They were both eaten by sharks.

The Scum's Party

I decided I'd have a big party
And I thought I'd invite all the scum.
I didn't even know what scum looked like
And didn't know if they would come.

I sent all the invites and prepared for the day
I bought lots of good food and drink
I cleaned all the house and made everything nice
But I don't really know how scum think.

Then at last the fatal day had arrived
And I saw the scum start to appear
They all seemed to look fairly reasonable
Perhaps there was nothing to fear.

But soon things began to get noisy
They said they were just having fun
But when they starting to wreck my place
I thought what on earth have I done?

There was scum in the lounge and the kitchen
There was scum in the bedrooms too
There was scum in the hall and the bathroom
What on earth was I going to do?

There was a horrible smell all over the house
Their actions were disgusting to see
The language they used was appalling.
And the scum wouldn't listen to me.

The male scum were really disgraceful
I just couldn't believe what I saw –
But the lady scum, oh my goodness
You should see what they did on the floor.

Above all the stench and the awful smoke
Their sickening behaviour and din.
The filth and damage and loss of control
There were more scum trying to get in.

I realised I had made a dreadful mistake
You cannot be nice to scum
I wanted it all to come to an end
Just why had I acted so dumb?

Then the strangest thing started to happen.
The scum were beginning to fall
There were piles of scum all over my house
I just had to step over it all.

It took a long time to clear all the filth.
Yes – my house will once more be okay.
But if I should live for a hundred years
I will never forget this scum day.

So if you're thinking of having a party
And you have any scum down your way
Just be careful when you write your invites
And make sure the damned scum stay away.

Have You Ever Been Really Frightened?

A few words on the Propagation and Psychology of Fear

We saw the men from a distance. We were ordered to keep marching and under no circumstance turn our heads. We knew better than to try. However I am sure that like mine, every pair of eyes were glancing to the left. What we saw was frightening: a group of between ten and twelve men were sprawled by the side of the building, some retching some holding their chests, some holding their throats. It looked like they were not able to see either. We wanted to help, but were quickly marched past. We had already endured what we considered acts of bad treatment whilst here. But the big dread was still to come. People were having nightmares and losing sleep. Sleep wasn't easy to come by anyway. Some were planning to escape or maybe try to go sick. None of these things would work however – they had all been tried before. The dreaded morning arrived. The notice was posted. Our names were there – all twelve of us. I was glad in a way – the waiting had been terrible.

We were marched off, all knowing full well what our destination was. The block building at the far side of the camp now came into view. We were quick-marching now, and being closely observed, there was to be no escape. The building was about four yards square. It was of a concrete construction with one wide external door. We were lined up outside. The first sign of compassion or concern was then shown to us.

'When inside you will be ordered to run on the spot, do it, it will make things easier. Under no circumstances hold your breath – this will increase your suffering and delay the end.'

We were all now resigned to our fate and ushered into the chamber. Inside was a small table. All eyes focused on the canister in the middle of the table. The external door thudded closed. It could only be opened from the outside. The only light was from a very low-wattage bulb on the ceiling. We were then ordered to start running on the spot. There was just about enough room to do this – even though we were packed like sardines.

The room was airtight and the remaining air was being rapidly used up. The effort of running had made us all pant, in fact we were dragging for air. The canister was then activated. Gas is of course invisible, but this had an agent added so we could see it. Gas expands to fill the surrounding volume; we could clearly see it reaching for every corner. Our last order about not holding our breath was difficult to ignore, but I was determined that I wouldn't hold mine. Some did however and their suffering was worse. I put my top lip over my bottom lip and tried to breathe in a shallow way. The pain was instantaneous; this was undiluted gas. My mouth and throat felt as if they were on fire; my lungs were thumping; my eyes felt as if they were melting. We should have closed our eyes, but we could not. I am sure everyone in that room was praying to God at that time, whether they believed in him or not.

After what seemed like an eternity, but in reality was perhaps a very short time, the door was opened. Those who were able to tumbled out and collapsed on the ground outside. Some had to be dragged out. We were not to be allowed the privilege of lying on the ground; we were dragged to our feet and ordered to run. We staggered for perhaps four hundred yards. This of course was the best thing to do – although we didn't realise it at the time. We needed the gas out of our lungs and air in as quickly as possible. Eventually those who were able were marched back to the building.

We then heard the order: 'Don't turn your heads or look at these men.'

That order was not directed at us though – it was directed at the men marching past. These men would have been watching us out of the corners of their eyes, regarding us with both pity and dread as we were rolling about holding ourselves.

Where did this happen? It happened whilst I was doing my National Service over fifty years ago.

During a later military exercise I sustained an injury which caused me difficulty walking. How grateful I was for that injury. It saved me from a repeat visit to the dreaded chamber, which my comrades had to endure for a second time.

Opportunities

How dumb the tongue that will not speak
When words just need to be said
How deaf the ears that will not hear
When words of forgiveness are aired.

How tense the hand that will not touch
When that's all it takes to go on
How closed the nose that will not smell
When aromas around are so strong.

How tight the mouth that will not taste
The flavours that lay on the tongue
How weak the legs that will not move
When the race is there to be won.

How blind the eye that will not see
The child or the dog at play
How foolish the man who dares to think
That he is here to stay.

Peace

A feeling of peace within?
Remember they have troubles too.
Cuddling close for protection and warmth,
Do you still hold the same view?

You seem agitated and I wonder at what,
Like the black notes on a score.
Making sense to some, but not to others,
There is no need for you to be at war.

Was mother queen so surely crowned?
Self contained like some tight ball.
Still hovering like a raindrop overhead,
No hiding place in thoughts at all.

Alone amid the misty gleam of dawn
The sated birds have had their fill,
No purer scene the whole world round
Each breath a brush mark, still.

The melting stream begins again to flow,
And youthful maidens haste to sing and dance.
All peaceful and sprightly they, on show,
And still you seem to say, perchance.

*

But now the feet of busy people walking to and fro,
With always a problem, or something to say
A time to pause, to think, to dream!
And hope tomorrow brings another day.

www.ingramcontent.com/pod-product-compliance
Lightning Source LLC
Chambersburg PA
CBHW021009090426
42738CB00007B/721